Counselling for Anxiety Problems

Richard Hallam

SAGE Publications
London • Newbury Park • New Delhi

First published 1992
Reprinted 1993

 SAGE Publications Ltd
6 Bonhill Street
London EC2A 4PU

SAGE Publications Inc
2455 Teller Road
Newbury Park, California 91320

SAGE Publications India Pvt Ltd
32, M-Block Market
Greater Kailash – I
New Delhi 110 048

British Library Cataloguing in Publication Data

Hallam, Richard S.
  Counselling for Anxiety Problems. –
  (Counselling in Practice Series)
  I. Title   II. Series
  362.2

  ISBN 0–8039–8460–X
  ISBN 0–8039–8461–8 (pbk)

Library of Congress catalog card number 92–050479

Typeset by Mayhew Typesetting, Rhayader, Powys
Printed and bound in Great Britain by
Biddles Ltd, Guildford and King's Lynn

Problems

9.95   19839

Counselling in Practice

Series editor: Windy Dryden
Associate editor: E. Thomas Dowd

Counselling in Practice is a series of books developed especially for counsellors and students of counselling which provides practical, accessible guidelines for dealing with clients with specific, but very common, problems.

Counselling Survivors of Childhood Sexual Abuse
Claire Burke Draucker

Counselling with Dreams and Nightmares
Delia Cushway and Robyn Sewell

Counselling for Depression
Paul Gilbert

Counselling for Anxiety Problems
Richard Hallam

Career Counselling
Robert Nathan and Linda Hill

Counselling for Post-traumatic Stress Disorder
Michael J. Scott and Stephen G. Stradling

Counselling for Alcohol Problems
Richard Velleman

Contents

List of Tables

List of Figures

Preface

All of us can empathize with what it might be like to suffer from an 'anxiety problem'. For example, in the first encounter with a client, a counsellor might worry about acting incompetently. The client, in turn, might be concerned about getting along with the counsellor. There may be a lurking fear that opening up too much could lead to an uncontrollable display of emotion. These relatively minor anxieties are not 'problems'. They are routinely faced and managed in counselling. However, they are similar to larger problems with respect to the content of the underlying worries and, when analysed in detail, they can appear just as complex. Both involve social expectations, self-evaluation, and some idea, however sketchy, of what *could* 'go wrong'.

Threat, worry and anxiety enter all forms of counselling, and special techniques are not necessarily needed to resolve them. Severe, persistent and irrational anxieties, however, call for more specialized methods. The purpose of this manual is to summarize, in the form of practical wisdom, what has been learned about anxiety, phobias and panic by clinical researchers and professionals working with clients. Most of the material has been described in scientific journals devoted to cognitive and behavioural therapies but these articles rarely describe hands-on experience or give the practical tips so useful to novices. This has been done more successfully in a number of detailed anxiety manuals (see Appendix A). The present short manual aims for broad coverage, an eclectic approach and a concise description of general principles. For ease of reading, factual and theoretical points are not backed up in the text by reference to academic sources, although each chapter is followed by suggestions for further reading. The manual will inevitably reflect my personal style of working; in mitigation, the hope is expressed that over a number of years of counselling anxiety problems, I will have learned something useful to pass on. This experience has also yielded a number of case illustrations for the manual, in which all personal details have been suitably disguised.

Regarding the personal element, two biases may become evident. First is my belief that clients are dependent (as we all are) on a limited vocabulary of terms to describe their psychological distress. There are a fair number of anxiety words – worry, tension, panic, unease, horror and so on – but none of them has precise referents. Clients struggle to find the words to describe their distressing experiences and commonly fall back on metaphor. Put another way, anxiety as an emotion (if it can be described as such) is not transparent. Clients may have difficulty in translating into words a complex web of associations, images, self-judgements, and half-formulated intuitions of threat. For instance, the statement 'I feel I am walking a minefield to a precipice' invites the counsellor to enquire what will explode, with what consequences, and with what inevitability and finality. As in counselling generally, the counsellor is helping the client to reframe experience and to reconstrue the self and the world in relation to past, present and future. The experiences to which anxiety refers centre around unpleasant sensations and happenings, real or imaginary. Given that what is unpleasant is not always easy to bring into conscious awareness, an anxiety problem may express itself in silence or in other forms of inhibition, in behaviour performed for no 'obvious' reason, or in a bodily symptom. In short, the client does not necessarily complain of 'anxiety'.

My second bias is to avoid prescriptive remedies for anxiety problems. Principles and techniques will be described in as abstract and flexible a manner as a practical manual allows. It cannot be stressed too strongly that all anxiety problems have some idiosyncratic feature that needs to be taken into consideration. In any event, techniques are employed in the context of a *process* of counselling with its different stages. It is assumed that anyone using this manual possesses basic counselling skills and would not attempt to apply techniques in a mechanical way. Although this manual is not a general introduction to the theory and practice of cognitive-behavioural counselling, I have devoted a considerable amount of space to providing a theoretical framework for assessing and formulating problems. This background is essential to provide the counsellor with a source of ideas for innovative solutions to anxiety problems. It is also important in the educative role the counsellor inevitably plays. The very notion of a manual implies that problems can be solved by the systematic application of technique. However, I believe that a technology should always be employed in the services of a form of counselling that views and responds to the client at a multiplicity of levels. A technical approach to overcoming habits of thought and behaviour is merely one of them.

The word counselling is derived from the verb to counsel or give advice. Some of the methods I describe depart significantly from this mode of influence. They require the counsellor to induce the client to face up to frightening thoughts or situations. Although the client's agreement and collaboration is always sought, the counsellor may feel responsible for the distress this procedure may cause. It should be expected that there will be times when the client cries or does not wish to continue with a procedure. Careful advance planning of the session makes this unlikely but there is probably no way of counselling anxiety problems which does not distress the client to some degree. Reservations about these methods decline as both counsellor and client realize the benefit they can bring. The client will feel most at ease if the counsellor is confident that progress is possible. Patience and calm determination are qualities for the counsellor to model. The counsellor straddles the divide between providing support and reassurance, and encouraging, leading, or even pushing the client to confront new challenges and frightening situations. Getting the balance right is not always easy. It is recommended that counsellors new to this area of work arrange regular support and advice from an experienced supervisor.

The manual is structured as follows. The first three chapters provide a theoretical framework and overview of the approach. This is followed by chapters on the formulation and assessment of anxiety problems. Some strategies are common to all forms of fear and anxiety, and these are described next. The most commonly encountered problems are those in which panic attacks play a major part. The longest chapter is therefore devoted to the topic of panic and associated phobias. Pervasive forms of anxiety related to worry and social anxiety are considered separately. The manual ends with a discussion of obstacles to progress. Clearly, anxiety problems cannot be neatly separated off from other life problems. This manual simply focuses on those aspects of a person's difficulties that are experienced as anxiety. The reader is directed to other manuals in this series dealing with related topics such as post-traumatic stress and depression.

Acknowledgements

I would like to give special thanks to Rosemarie Archer for reading the developing manuscript and for the innumerable helpful suggestions she made. I also thank Windy Dryden for his good advice at various stages.

For Sophie May

1

A Theoretical Framework for Anxiety Problems

To counsel anxiety problems effectively, it is necessary to have a good theoretical understanding of the topic. In this chapter I will consider the term anxiety as a linguistic concept and differentiate the process of *naming* distress in this way from processes that *give rise* to distress. I will conclude the chapter with a review of the biological contribution to anxiety problems.

What is anxiety?

We tend to use the term 'anxiety' without examining its meaning too closely. We use it of other people even when they deny acting anxiously. We sometimes use it to explain our own behaviour after it has occurred ('I must have been anxious'). In my opinion, anxiety should not be regarded as something that *exists*, causing all the phenomena we refer to as anxiety. Instead, we can view it as an everyday word which refers, in a shorthand fashion, to what is in reality a complex relationship occurring through time between a person and the situation he or she faces. It can refer to (1) the behavioural and physiological responses directly induced by a situation; (2) an appraisal of the responses and their effects; (3) a person's intentions towards a situation; and (4) a person's evaluation of the resources available for dealing with it. The situation is likely to be an unpleasant one (or signal some future unpleasantness) but our gift for imagining unpleasantness can be so well developed that the anxiety-provoking nature of the situation is not always obvious. The salient marker of this complex relationship is how the person *feels*, but as noted earlier, the concept of anxiety is not always used to refer to a person's self-reported feelings.

If this view of anxiety is correct, (that it is an everyday construct which refers to more than just a subjective feeling), then it suggests that there is no single set of psychological or biological processes that define it uniquely. Anxiety cannot be understood in purely objective terms as a state of the organism. The concept is likely to be used in slightly different ways by different people, and the same

Table 1.1 *Common referents for anxiety words*

An unpleasant quality of subjective experience varying through 'tension' to 'terror'

An awareness of imminent danger or harm whether or not its sources can be specified

An experience of bodily sensations associated particularly with activation of the autonomic nervous system

A strong urge to flee to a place of safety

A lack of control over fine motor movements

Thoughts of a worrying or unpleasant nature over which there is little control

An inability to think clearly or act in a coordinated manner especially in novel, conflictual or threatening situations

---

NB: 'Anxiety' is inferred in *others* on the basis of (1) observing behaviour indicative of the above; (2) perception of the context as threatening or stressful; and (3) other signs such as facial expression and pitch of voice.

person might use it differently on separate occasions. In brief, the word anxiety, and terms with a related meaning, do a rough and ready job which suffices for most purposes. When pressed, a person will go on to supply a richer account of the situation, including a description of his/her intentions, perceptions of others, and perhaps mention a variety of sensations and feelings.

The common referents for anxiety words are listed in Table 1.1. Given the wide range of meaning, it is safe to say that a variety of psychological and biological processes are involved. Virtually all areas of theoretical psychology are relevant – innate biological defences, models of stress, self-conception, social evaluation, skill and competence, cognition, problem-solving, learning and so on.

Some implications of viewing anxiety as an everyday construct

Describing oneself as anxious is not just an academic exercise in naming a frame of mind; it also serves some purpose in social interaction. The unpleasantness of the experience to which it refers certainly captures the attention and helps to identify the presence of a problem. A failure to recognize 'anxiety' may leave a person unprepared as a situation unfolds. Communication of 'anxiety' prepares others for potential failure in joint enterprises. It also serves to enlist support. It is no accident that people with the most soothing manner are those we have come to trust completely, such as airline pilots. For them to communicate anxiety would amount to an admission that they expected to encounter problems that they could not handle. The voice quality is intended to reassure us that no assistance is needed.

A further assumption we can make is that the ability to name anxiety and communicate it verbally is *learned*. This implies that a *verbal/cognitive* process is operating to some extent independently of other processes that give rise to the experiences we construe as anxiety. Of course, once we have mastered a language and its concepts, information that is verbally transmitted can act as a potent stimulus for fearful behaviour. Information about what is likely to happen may terrify us. As we shall see, the tendency for biologically based responses to come under the control of symbolic processes (that is, thoughts, assumptions or interpretations), is one explanation for anxiety becoming a problem.

The verbal and cognitive abilities which enable us to name our emotions and account for them socially are influenced during their development by the sub-culture of the family and by the broader social milieu. Parents differ, for example, in the extent to which they draw the attention of their offspring to potential threats ('Don't *ever* talk to strange men') or to their bodily sensations and feelings ('You must be upset, you're so hot and bothered'). The child will become more or less sensitized by parental reminders, and by actual experiences, to those threats that most concern us in our culture. Besides the threats which appear to be part of our biological inheritance (darkness, heights, being stared at, small animals, and so on), there is another set of themes which constantly recur in anxiety problems. These relate to our physical survival (death, illness, material security) and to fears of the loss of others, social rejection and negative evaluation. The extent to which a person is willing or able to express concern about these threats varies a great deal and this variation is probably related to the 'emotion training' he or she has received as a child. It is widely accepted that boys and girls receive different kinds of emotion training.

The distinction I have drawn here between an everyday construct of emotion and that to which it refers has some interesting implications. On occasions, what a person says is or is not threatening and how that person behaves, are at odds with each other. A person may look tense and withdraw but deny feeling anxious. Another may worry incessantly about what *could* happen but do very little about it and regard their worrying as pointless. Another may feel nauseous or have heart palpitations in apparently stressful situations, but deny that the situation is threatening or that they feel anxious. These examples underline the complexity of anxiety problems. Although most researchers now accept that there can be gross discrepancies between the verbal/cognitive expression of 'anxiety' and other behavioural and physiological indicators of emotion, it is not so easy to explain them theoretically. There are many factors to consider but at this point I will look at some further implications of differentiating the 'emotion naming' process from 'what-is-named'.

Naming anxiety and the development of 'anxiety memories'

As we begin to make observations of our own behaviour and that of others, and use words to name and communicate these situations, the words themselves enter into and influence the events we are observing. They enter in a concrete way as sound patterns and come to be associated with other experienced elements in the situation. Just as a churchyard in the moonlight may be perceived as 'spooky', words also become evocative, through association with behavioural and physiological reaction to events, and acquire an emotional life of their own. A word, or a verbal description linking together the elements of a fearful event, is stored with the memory of that event, and helps to re-evoke it when a person is prompted by instruction or reverie to recall the event later on.

The sound patterns we know as words are of course richly associated with a huge number of concrete situations that we have personally experienced. They also enter as symbols in a language that allows us to reason, plan, order, categorize and so forth. One of the consequences of our ability to form verbal associations between events that are unrelated in time and place is our great potential 'to scare ourselves silly'. We become anxious or afraid when it is inappropriate or unwise to do so. One form of association is made on the basis of physical similarity to the stimuli which were elements in the original fear experience. This mechanism (*stimulus generalization*) operates on the physical properties of stimuli. A garden hose may be perceived as a snake: a siren of a certain pitch may evoke the memory of an air-raid warning. Written words with a similar physical structure might also evoke anxiety memories (for example, eyelash and car crash).

A second form of association is based on reasoning and logical inference. We might infer that since eating raw eggs has been known to produce salmonella poisoning, eating a lightly boiled egg could make us ill and cause our death. This is one form of *symbolic generalization*. It is clearly an essential cognitive ability to associate events on the basis of their abstract properties. In many cases, an inference is borne out by experience; at other times it is not, and our anticipatory anxiety proves to be unwarranted and unnecessary. Inferences about unpleasant events can be based on misinformation, or religious belief, or on widespread superstition. For these cases, the associations between representations of events in our memory is made for us by others and we absorb them unwittingly. A great deal of this culturally transmitted knowledge is of great value.

Another form of symbolic generalization involves identifying with the events depicted in a book or in a picture, or in events that we are witnessing before us. We take on the role of the other person and respond as if the events were happening to us.

Anxiety memories have been conceptualized as a network of associations between representations of the situation, of responses to it, and of semantic links between them. There are features of these anxiety memories that predispose us to develop anxiety problems. As the memory is re-evoked by circumstances or voluntary recall, the associations between elements may strengthen and new links may form on the basis of generalization as described above. It may require less and less of a stimulus to evoke the memory, and as time goes on, all elements of the network are evoked together when only one element is stimulated. For example, anxiety memories include representations of the stimulus input from bodily arousal such as rapid heartbeats, irregular breathing, sweating and trembling. These stimulus elements can be evoked by normal daily activities such as running upstairs or drinking a strong cup of coffee. Bodily arousal produced by exercise is similar to bodily arousal associated with anxiety. As a result, anxiety memories tend to be evoked by exercise. Once evoked, other elements of the anxiety memory are retrieved and recalled, such as 'This rapid pulse could mean I'm having a heart attack.' An innocuous experience can therefore give rise to full-blown terror.

It might be supposed that all that a person needs to do to overcome an anxiety problem is to recognize how their anxiety memories are constructed and to dissociate those elements that are illogical or cannot be validated by real-life experience. This view contains more than a grain of truth but it ignores several aspects of our psychology that argue against it. These concern the role of *awareness*, the formation of *habits*, the presence of extreme *mood* states, *physical* and *personality* factors.

Awareness

The associative connections of an anxiety memory are not always available for examination. For instance, there are deeply embedded cultural beliefs about the connections between events (for example, what happens after death, what 'madness' signifies) which may be accepted without ever being consciously examined; they may not even be accessible to formulations by conscious reasoning. Some associations are merely pre-conscious in the sense that by careful questioning a counsellor can elicit them. A situation might be associated with a fleeting image such as the visual image of a burst blood vessel. However, a client may find the associated thought or image difficult to describe because it occurs so briefly in fragmented form and appears so illogical. The accessibility of pre-conscious associations can sometimes be facilitated by a guided fantasy conducted during deep relaxation or in hypnotic trance. Completely unexpected associations can arise when anxiety memories are vividly recalled, especially when the client is in large measure reliving the remembered experiences. For instance, a man who had a fear of 'sleep paralysis' (a state occasionally reported on waking in which the 'mind is awake' while the body remains in its paralysed sleeping state), recalled during guided fantasy several events from his past that were associated with the fear that sleep paralysis produced in him. While paralysed, he was unable to speak and he felt trapped in a no man's land of non-existence. One image he recalled concerned entrapment: that of being almost strangled as an adolescent by the vice-like grip of another boy with whom he was fighting.

One account of the relative inaccessibility of these kinds of image is that they are so unpleasant that active defensive processes keep them repressed. Another possibility is that they are remote childhood memories that were not verbally encoded at the time (because the child cannot articulate its experiences) and are therefore difficult to retrieve.

Habit

The associative connections between the elements of anxiety memories are likely to be strengthened every time a person re-experiences their 'anxiety'. For example, a 'panic attack' (see chapter 7), which may continue for several minutes in a highly unpleasant manner until the person escapes to a place of safety, simply strengthens the associations between all the elements involved (bodily sensations, frightening thoughts, aspects of the environment, running away, and so on). Moreover, once the 'panic attack' has been encoded as an unpleasant experience to be avoided at all costs, any sign that the panic will recur is associated with the attack and becomes a new element in the memory. The more that anxiety becomes a dominant concern of the person, the more the external and internal (bodily) environment will be scanned to check for warning signs that another panic is imminent. For this reason a person may become preoccupied with their bodily sensations, or avoid places where they think panic will occur.

It is generally assumed that an anxiety memory is maintained (and gradually encompasses more and more elements) because a person *avoids* deliberately evoking or recalling it. A person escapes from a distressing situation and attempts to put an end to fearful imagery. Any activity that leads to 'anxiety' is avoided in order to maintain a sense of safety. The memory is therefore protected from new experiences that could help to change it in a positive direction.

It is not surprising that as an anxiety problem grows in strength it becomes a habit that is hard to break. It comes to be seen as irrational because the degree of distress experienced is disproportional to any obvious source of threat. In comparison to his/her rational judgements of what is a 'normal' or 'appropriate' degree of anxiety, the person begins to perceive him or herself as 'silly', 'neurotic', or 'out of control'.

One mechanism, then, for the growth of an anxiety problem is the steady addition of new warning signals (that is, through associations between new situations and instances of 'anxiety') and a failure to test out reality (that is, escaping or avoiding when the warning signal occurs). A second mechanism appears to involve a vicious cycle (see chapter 2). A vicious cycle is created when the person's response to anxiety, instead of improving matters, reinstates the conditions that gave rise to it. For reasons already stated, simply understanding what might have caused an anxiety problem is not sufficient to break into this vicious cycle. Behavioural techniques that involve the breaking of habits are usually required.

Mood

The more that an anxious or depressed mood predominates, the greater the difficulty the client has of mobilizing positive thinking and constructive defences. In extreme cases, negative thinking seriously hinders attempts to reframe a client's perception of his/her situation. People who continually worry always seem able to find a new threat to concern them or an additional reason for disbelieving evidence that a situation is not as dangerous as it seems. In some cases, negative thinking appears to be irrefutable: we all eventually die and prior to that illness may cause hardship and suffering. However, even these hard realities can be reconstrued, especially when there is no evidence that the client has been singled out for a worse lot than anyone else.

Clients who are severely agitated or depressed may require a broader range of interventions, including medication, and may require more intensive or prolonged counselling. However, the methods described in this manual still apply. Careful thought should be given to the order of interventions. A client is unlikely to make progress with a specific anxiety problem when, for example, a source of safety is lacking, when lack of assertion is creating problems in job or relationships, or when a chronic major stressor is impinging on a client's life. Generally speaking, these problems should be addressed first or, at least, concurrently.

Physical factors

The client's medical history should always be investigated and whenever doubt about physical disorder remains, the client should be referred back to a physician. Many anxiety problems are complicated by the presence of physical impairments. These can be as simple as poor vision or as obviously important as a hormonal disorder. It is important that the client correctly attribute his/her psychological state to physical factors when these are known to be influential. Information about a physical condition can be reassuring when unusual sensations are experienced, or the seriousness of the condition is misunderstood. In some cases, treatable medical problems are identified. A list of physical factors of which a counsellor should be aware is given in Table 1.2.

A common problem in anxious clients is that of over-breathing, which can give rise to a cluster of effects called the *hyperventilation syndrome*. The effects themselves can be extremely variable. They are caused by a change in the proportion of oxygen and carbon dioxide in the blood and are benign. As this is an important topic in its own right (some theorists maintain that hyperventilation syndrome accounts for most anxiety problems), it will be dealt with in detail later (see chapter 7). Treatment programmes have been devised to teach a slower rate of respiration and an increased dependence on diaphragmatic rather than thoracic breathing.

Personality

Relatively little is known about the personality characteristics that predispose a person to develop an anxiety problem. There is, however, growing evidence for the existence of a genetic predisposition to anxiety problems. This genetic vulnerability does not always manifest itself as a lifelong trait. Panic attacks are rarely observed in children, and many adults who develop them have never regarded themselves as 'nervous individuals.'

Anxiety problems involve a multitude of psychological processes and so the way they present themselves can reflect many features

Table 1.2 *Major physical disorders that can produce symptoms experienced as anxiety**

Hormonal disorders	
Hyperthyroidism	resulting from excess thyroid hormone
Hypoparathyroidism	resulting from decreased secretion of parathyroid hormone
Cushing's syndrome	resulting from increased circulating cortisol
Pheochromocytoma	a rare tumour causing excessive catecholamine (adrenaline and noradenaline) secretion
Hypoglycaemia	an acute or chronic form of low blood sugar which may produce weakness, sweating, faintness, tremor, etc.
Temporal lobe epilepsy	sensations may result from cortical electrical discharges
Cardiovascular disorders	resulting in perception of heartbeat and heart-rate irregularities
Balance disorders	resulting in dizziness, nausea, unsteadiness or falling

* See also McCue and McCue (1984).

of a client's personality. The adaptations a person makes to an anxiety problem should not be mistaken for its cause. For instance, independent and outgoing persons can become withdrawn and dependent as a result of experiencing a series of severe panic attacks.

I have already noted the great significance of thought, reasoning and judgement in the evocation of anxiety problems. For this reason, the following aspects of the client's personality will influence the outcome of counselling; the ability to make correct attributions, to think flexibly rather than in a dichotomous black and white fashion, to suppress thoughts about improbable unpleasant outcomes, to tolerate uncertainty and to make accurate self-appraisals. In large measure, a counsellor is helping the client to develop these abilities. This should become apparent as individual case histories are discussed.

Biological aspects of anxiety problems

The arguments for a biological basis to many aspects of anxiety problems look strong. Mammals respond to the threat of a predator or the invasion of territory in ways that look similar across genera and species. This apparent similarity conceals considerable variation. Flight and attack are the two main forms of defence, and the two response patterns may alternate. The physiological changes that occur in the body to prepare the individual for either defence are quite similar. We can see this alternation in clients with anxiety problems as well; there may be conflict between running away from a threatening situation and a tendency to get angry with the person or thing (or with oneself) that is perceived as the source of threat.

In humans, the rational appraisal of information powerfully influences the expression of simple 'instinctive reactions'. Nevertheless, in very frightening situations we react reflexively in ways over which we have little control; we might scream or evacuate our bowels. Even under mildly stressful situations such as the threat of missing a train, we tend 'to get in a panic', unable to think clearly about how to get from one platform to another.

There are different views on how the biological and learned (mainly cultural) aspects of anxiety problems are related to each other. One view is that culture merely acts to select one 'basic' emotional response or another. A more satisfactory view is that this is a two-way relationship, which assumes that far more of what we consider as 'instinctive emotional reactions' are in fact learned in social interaction. This applies especially to anxiety problems which lack the obvious behavioural markers of fear. Put differently, anxiety problems involve the whole person in his/her social context. They do so because the polarity of safety and danger acts as a backcloth to much of human activity. People constantly seek safety and security in order to counter the real or imagined threats of poverty, ill-health, ecological disaster, old age, and so forth.

From a biological standpoint, the range of behavioural response patterns that span the safety–danger continuum can be divided into three zones: safety, vigilance and imminent threat responses. We will consider each in turn.

Safety

A safe base is essential if threat is to be confronted successfully. In infancy, the young child explores away from the parent. In adulthood, a sense of safety is derived from many sources – for example a secure relationship, a home base, close friends, a job that provides financial security. When dealing with an anxiety problem, the counsellor implicitly offers him/herself as a buttress to the client's sense of safety. In methods which involve helping the client to confront directly a threatening situation, the counsellor explicitly provides a safe base. A *safety signal* is the technical term applied to a stimulus that reduces the amount of defensive behaviour in a fearful situation. Safety signals operate in at least two ways:

First, the signal indicates that the threat is less likely or less severe. For instance, in the presence of the counsellor, the client thinks more rationally about the real danger and is reassured by the counsellor's assessment of threat. Alternatively, the client may feel safe when wearing a charm or carrying out some ritual which in the past has been associated with the absence of threat. Anything which realistically or superstitiously reduces the magnitude or likelihood of something unpleasant happening can function as a safety signal.

Second, the safety signal has the property of reducing defensive responses directly. Strictly speaking, it is not a signal but a suppressant. The 'arm over the shoulders' is the conventional way of soothing a troubled person. Touch is rarely employed by counsellors (because it may give out the wrong signals and risks being experienced as unpleasant), but it has a place at some moments of counselling. Other safety signals of this type include responses which compete with fearful defensiveness. Eating, acting angrily or deliberately relaxing have all been employed therapeutically in this way. The process has been referred to as *reciprocal inhibition*.

To conclude, certain features of anxiety problems can be interpreted as safety-seeking. Clients may explain simply that they feel safer when wearing dark glasses, carrying a bottle of tranquillizers (even if never used) or pushing a shopping trolley. The counsellor should attempt to discover the main sources of the client's sense of safety and security and build on these where possible. A companion or helper may be called in for specific purposes to provide a bridge between safety and danger until the client acquires sufficient self-confidence to proceed alone. As mentioned earlier, a client needs to have a safety anchor point from which to explore and confront threat. When these anchors are fundamentally threatened (for instance by redundancy, homelessness, marital breakdown, legal prosecution), the counsellor is best directed towards helping to resolve these practical problems as the first priority.

Vigilance
Between safety and danger lies a large grey zone of potential threat combined with uncertainty about the best course of action. Anyone who has watched birds feeding on scattered breadcrumbs will have noticed an alternation between the consumption of food and a scanning of the environment for potential movement or sound. Flight ensues beyond a certain threshold of stimulus change. Similarly, a snake phobic who is being asked, for therapeutic reasons, to confront a live snake is likely to alternate between a

relaxed posture and a posture of fear expressed by slight crouching, hunched shoulders, eyes fixed on the threat, and an obvious readiness to flee. This posture is also seen in the nervous client who sits on the edge of a chair. In these examples, we see a readiness to employ an escape manoeuvre. Escape and other defensive responses are associated with physiological changes in the body that contribute to the experience of anxiety.

The pattern of response in a vigilant state differs slightly from the response to immediate danger. The event that threatens has not yet occurred and there is uncertainty as to when it will occur, how bad it will be, and whether it will be possible to deal adequately with it. The organism is attentive to all stimulus changes and responds by orientation to the source of change. There is an increased readiness to startle and orientation to stimulus change or signs of threat momentarily stops the organism in its tracks. The heart rate slows down and peripheral blood vessels constrict, resisting the flow of blood, thereby increasing blood pressure. These physiological changes function to prepare the organism for defensive action; blood flow is increased to the skeletal muscles and glucose and fatty acids are released from tissue as energy sources.

What is noteworthy about the state of vigilance, thinking of this in terms of anxiety problems, is the persistent alertness and repeated inhibition of the stream of behaviour. Behaviour lacks smoothness, muscles are tense, attention to irrelevant information affects memory and concentration. Breathing is irregular, and digestive, excretory and sexual functions are affected. These changes are largely the result of activation of the *sympathetic branch* of the *autonomic nervous system*. They prepare the organism for vigorous action. They underlie the complaints of many anxious clients.

The startle reaction may be elicited by any sudden stimulus change. However, if the nature of the threat is understood, attention will be directed specifically at signs of the known threat. A snake phobic will tend to look at wiggly bits of rope, and so forth. In anxiety problems, illness or insanity are often perceived as the root source of threat. This means that clients are likely to watch out for signs of abnormality in their bodily sensations, reactions or mental processes. Unfortunately, an over-attentiveness to the self may disrupt the smooth flow of behaviour and produce physiological reactions that themselves are perceived as abnormal. This can create a vicious circle and thus perpetuate an anxiety problem.

Preparedness for action may break out in restless movement, fidgeting, pacing or foot tapping. The primary complaint of the client may be that of muscle tension and an inability to relax. Insomnia may accompany this hyper-aroused state.

We know from surveys of patients in general practice clinics that it is an *impending* danger or *threatened* disruption in a person's life that is most closely associated with a complaint of anxiety. By contrast, a depressed mood is more likely to follow the loss of something valued (such as one's health) rather than the threat of this loss. An important part of the counsellor's task is to enhance the sense of safety by helping the client conceptualize the threat, prepare for it and, where possible, neutralize it. The threat may be too awful to think about; however, until the threat is grasped intellectually, little can be done by way of preparation. The mental work of describing threats, naming them and appraising options can dramatically reduce a client's distress.

Imminent threat
At this point I will consider the variety of fear responses to imminent threat and also survey our biological predisposition to regard certain kinds of stimulus as fearful.

Fear responses   In mammals, including humans, we see two main types of fear reaction:

- The response of freezing and becoming mute;
- The response of being startled, screaming, and running away.

The second reaction is more familiar but we also talk of being 'scared stiff' or 'frozen in fear'. In the latter case, the individual is unable to move (although the paralysis of the muscles may be short-lived), the body may tremble and feel cold, numb and insensitive to pain, and there is an inability to call out or scream.

A strong fear of the second type can be defined by the cluster of features outlined in Table 1.3. Not all of these features are present simultaneously; some may follow others in a sequential pattern, and fear may alternate with aggression. A large element in the subjective experience of fear is of course the perception of profound bodily change produced by the action of the autonomic nervous system. The sensations described by clients as fear, panic or anxiety are very broad indeed, including blurred vision, a feeling of faintness, difficulty in breathing and many more. Sometimes the subjective feeling of terror is uppermost, sometimes the urge to escape, and sometimes the awareness of unpleasant bodily reactions and sensations. All these aspects of fear/anxiety can occur separately as well as together. A client might say that he or she is

Table 1.3   *Strong fear – flight response*

Feeling of terror
Urge to run and hide
Crying out
Pounding heart
Rising blood pressure
Tense muscles
Rapid breathing
Pale sweaty skin
Hair standing on end
Dryness of throat and mouth
Sinking feeling in stomach
Tendency to urinate/defecate
Dilating pupils
Tingling of hands/feet
Weakness of the limbs
Sense of faintness or falling

panicking while apparently sitting calmly in a chair. Another might deny feeling anxious, while showing behavioural or physiological signs of fear.

Fear-evoking stimuli Different species of mammals are predisposed to fear different situations. The range of fears can be understood in terms of the environment in which the species evolved. All environments pose certain physical threats and there is threat too from other animals, including members of the same species. The threats to which humans appear to be biologically predisposed are listed in Table 1.4. A predisposition of this kind is not necessarily expressed to the same degree in all people, and a predisposed fear can be overcome by familiarity and mastery.

It is likely that many of the fears of infants are related to the predispositions sketched above. Moreover, before a rational adult outlook is achieved, children are more easily influenced by frightening symbolic information such as stories of ghosts or images of horror. Infant-fears usually disappear in the pre-school years, but some (such as fear of animals) begin to become more prevalent and then die away later. Many adult fears and phobias can be dated back to childhood. A fear of strangers may persist as shyness. A fear of blood and injury or small animals often originates in childhood. Detailed questioning sometimes reveals a particularly unpleasant experience at an early age. For instance, an infant strapped in its buggy is liable to have a dog jump up and

Table 1.4 *Biological predispositions to threat*

Physical threats
   Extreme cold and heat
   Very loud sounds
   Sudden loss of support
   Pain
   Heights
   Bright, open spaces
   Darkness
   Confinement in small enclosed spaces
   New, unknown, objects, places or sensations
   Sudden movements
   Small animals (such as snakes/spiders)

Social threats
   Strangers (especially in infants 8–24 months)
   Touch/proximity (unfamiliar persons)
   Being looked at (especially staring eyes)
   Being alone (especially unaccompanied young children)

bark at it. An experience like this can perpetuate a fear of animals that would otherwise have died away.

An imminent danger does not of itself produce a strong defensive reaction of this biological type. We are taught from an early age how to avoid harm, how to resist hostility, how to deflect criticism. It has been suggested that in any potentially threatening situation we make an immediate appraisal of the size of the threat and the resources we have for dealing with it. This need not be a deliberate, reflective appraisal although, at times, consciously thinking about threat may come into it. Emotional responses to threat such as attack or flight can be viewed as rearguard actions when threat cannot be circumvented or mastered by the cool exercise of skill and judgement.

A constant state of readiness to flee or freeze is not a frame of mind in which a person can easily conduct their daily affairs. The features of a threat that are most likely to produce this unpleasant degree of preparedness are related to uncertainties:

- There is uncertainty about the nature of the threat or how severe it might be;
- There is uncertainty about if and when the threat will become an imminent reality;
- There is uncertainty about whether one has the skills or material/emotional resources to counter the threat;

- There is conflict over the options available for dealing with the threat;
- There is uncertainty about the harmful secondary (knock-on) consequences of failing to deal with the threat.

Uncertainty militates against preparedness, and preparedness can be conceptualized as foreknowledge of how and when one will achieve safety. Anxiety implies hope of success because a *certain*, *uncontrollable* threat is likely to be faced with resignation and despair.

A further complication here is that for some people, expressing fear is interpreted as a sign that they are losing control of themselves, going mad or making a fool of themselves. Amongst the consequences of failing to control a threat, then, is the feared possibility of some injury to one's psychological integrity or self-esteem. The effects of expressing fear are themselves feared. As we shall see later, this is an important aspect of anxiety problems.

Suggestions for further reading

A comprehensive survey of theoretical and treatment approaches to anxiety problems has been produced by Barlow (1988). A short concise overview of the field can also be found in Warren and Zgourides (1991). Rachman (1990) offers a readable introduction to the topic, including theoretical issues. Useful edited volumes giving a variety of perspectives include Tuma and Maser (1985), Last and Hersen (1988) and Michelson and Ascher (1987). The concept of safety signals has been discussed by Himadi (1987) and Rachman (1984). The biological aspects of anxiety have been thoroughly reviewed by Marks (1987). For a contrasting linguistic/contextual viewpoint see Smail (1984).

2

Genesis of Anxiety Problems

The everyday concept of anxiety refers to processes that are essential for our survival. Occasionally, 'normal anxiety' gets in the way of thinking clearly or of acting in a coordinated manner but, in general, the apprehension of threat, experienced as unpleasant, spurs a person on to prepare effectively and counter the threat. The question I will now consider is why it is that anxiety becomes persistent, excessive and unhelpful. The question has no simple answer because 'anxiety' refers to a complex set of circumstances and experiences with multiple causes. Some of the processes that are thought to lead to problematic anxiety are considered below.

One important feature of human behaviour which runs throughout psychological explanations is our reflexive observation of our own selves. That is, it appears that as our actions unfold, as if spontaneously, a part of the self is observing, commenting on and directing those actions. For instance, we might blush at a social gaffe, think about how this might be perceived by an observer and then, in the light of this, respond to the knowledge that we have blushed. A complex sequence of reactions ensues involving at times vicious cycles that intensify our original discomfort. The blush, instead of fading, deepens; we might leave the situation and subsequently find it difficult to return.

In this example there are immediate and longer-term consequences of the initial reaction. It is usually some combination of immediate and longer-term consequences that accounts for

the spread of an anxiety problem from an initial focus; and its persistence over time.

How a person deals with threat and how they react to the consequences of their attempts to deal with it are therefore crucial.

Consider first how an anxiety-provoking situation is successfully confronted and eventually comes to be regarded as safe. Public speaking is a good example of a situation that is feared by most people. When asked to give a speech, a person goes through the following steps in successfully meeting the request:

1 Acknowledging that public speaking represents a real though manageable threat – that it is not denied or minimized out of existence ('This is really no problem for me at all') nor exaggerated so much that confronting it is unimaginable ('You'd never get me up there in front of an audience');
2 Confronting it – either by rehearsing public speaking to develop one's self-confidence, or by simply gritting one's teeth and going ahead;
3 Evaluating the success or otherwise of the result;
4 Repeating step 2, with perhaps some modification of approach in light of the evaluation made in step 3.

Most of us have successfully gone through these steps whether as a public speaker, in learning to swim, or in getting to know someone who seems forbidding. Admittedly, public speaking is a fairly straightforward example. An anxiety problem that is related to, say, a fear of death or a decision to separate from a partner represents a different challenge. Nevertheless, one can see how in both of these cases a failure to go through the steps outlined above might generate an anxiety problem. Threats that are not acknowledged or realistically appraised cannot call forth an appropriate response. Objects, situations or mental images that are repeatedly avoided cannot be confronted and mastered. A reluctance to tolerate some degree of discomfort blocks new learning. An inability to evaluate progress positively undermines motivation.

These are elementary obstacles which take many forms in anxiety problems. A key to effective counselling is finding ways of successfully circumventing these obstacles. The emphasis shifts from individual to individual, between types of problems, and across time. Thus, priority may be given first to appraisal – such as recognizing what the threat consists of, or estimating personal resources, or evaluating irrational beliefs in catastrophic outcomes. Later the emphasis may switch to the threatening situation – breaking it down into smaller, manageable tasks, allowing confrontation to proceed. Finally, counselling might focus on self-evaluation and motivation for change.

Some manuals use the term 'anxiety management' as if anxiety was an entity like a fever, which has to be brought under control. Relaxation training is sometimes thought of in this way – as an antidote comparable to aspirin. It is true that some interventions are designed to modify behaviour directly but this is for the purpose of breaking into vicious cycles (see p. 67) that may be perpetuating a problem. The emphasis in this manual is on changing the *causes* of anxiety rather than managing anxiety viewed as a psychological disorder.

Processes that produce or maintain anxiety problems

It is not useful to conceive of anxiety simply as a unitary emotional response to an identified threat. Our behaviour can become halting, disjointed or out of control for a variety of reasons and this state of affairs may be experienced as 'anxiety'. For example when a parent is suddenly bombarded with questions from children it may be impossible for the parent to function effectively until he/she has 'taken control' of themselves or the situation. It is certainly true that a person's distress may be compounded by a perception that the self is threatened (e.g. 'I am not coping as well as I should, therefore I am a useless person') but the underlying source of behavioural disorganization may be grounded in genuinely problematic circumstances. The piling on of threat to stress is often how the vicious cycle element of anxiety problems is introduced. It is not an easy matter to describe all the processes that potentially cause and maintain anxiety problems. Figure 2.1 is an attempt to single out different processes. Each one will be described in turn.

Chronic source of behavioural disorganization

The problem may lie in *external* or *internal* sources of disorganization. The most obvious external sources are threats which the individual feels helpless to control (e.g. loss of employment, breakdown of relationships, phobic situations). Other external sources of disorganization include conflicts and uncertainty about important lifetime decisions (such as the decision to marry or divorce), or illnesses that produce impairments and disabilities. Excessive demands placed on an individual by work or family commitments is another factor. Some disorganizing events are more subtle, such as the realization that important goals are unattainable or the loss of faith in a personal philosophy that helps to organize and structure an individual's life. Disorganization may be experienced in a number of ways, including prevarication, overarousal of the body, unpleasant bodily sensations, clumsiness, unsteadiness or simply a sense of unreality.

The sources of disorganization of primarily internal origin can be classified as follows.

1 *Maladaptive conceptualization of difficulties* Through strong

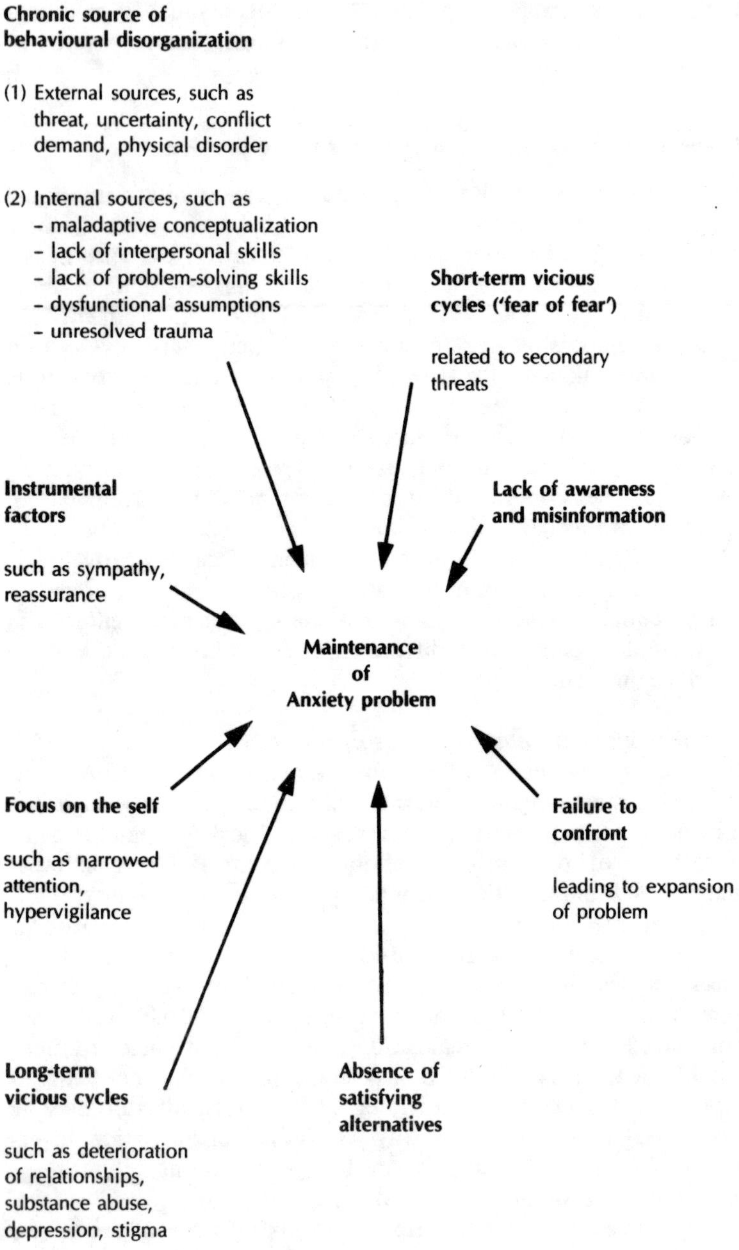

**Chronic source of
behavioural disorganization**

(1) External sources, such as
    threat, uncertainty, conflict
    demand, physical disorder

(2) Internal sources, such as
    – maladaptive conceptualization
    – lack of interpersonal skills
    – lack of problem-solving skills
    – dysfunctional assumptions
    – unresolved trauma

**Short-term vicious
cycles ('fear of fear')**

related to secondary
threats

**Instrumental
factors**

such as sympathy,
reassurance

**Lack of awareness
and misinformation**

**Maintenance
of
Anxiety problem**

Focus on the self

such as narrowed
attention,
hypervigilance

**Failure to
confront**

leading to expansion
of problem

**Long-term
vicious cycles**

such as deterioration
of relationships,
substance abuse,
depression, stigma

**Absence of
satisfying
alternatives**

Figure 2.1   *Processes that produce or maintain anxiety
problems*

personal convictions, a client may believe that the problem has its origin in a physical disorder; in attitudes to circumstances, past or present, which he or she does not wish to, or cannot, influence; in a defect of personality; and so on. When clients are unwilling to examine these convictions, there is little to offer.

2 Lack of problem-solving skills The client may not express a maladaptive conceptualization of his/her problem, yet lack an understanding of how it might be tackled constructively. Typically, the client is constantly 'stressed' and moves repeatedly from one life crisis to another. These clients may be helped by 'stress-management' or 'problem-solving' methods (see chapter 8) in which attention is given to identifying problems, setting priorities, breaking down problems into smaller components, comparing solutions and so on.

3 Lack of interpersonal skills The client may have difficulty in appraising social situations or lack skills for relating to other people (see chapter 8). A common problem is lack of assertion.

4 Dysfunctional assumption about self, others or the world The client has certain deeply held beliefs that lead him/her to judge situations in a rigid, absolute manner, thereby guaranteeing that self or others fail to match up to them. Everyday life becomes a constant source of dissatisfaction and disappointment (see chapter 8).

5 Unresolved trauma The origin of anxiety-provoking intrusive thoughts, upsetting images or other distressing emotions may lie in unresolved memories of traumatic events such as the death of a loved one, childhood abuse or wartime experiences. The counsellor can assist the client by using confrontational techniques (see chapter 6) adapted for this purpose; other manuals in this series deal more directly with these problems.

Short-term vicious cycles (fear of fear)

The various anomalous sensations and signs of behavioural disorganizations the client notices may become the source of what I refer to as *secondary threats* (see Table 2.1). The client responds to him/herself (or his/her image of self) and by so doing creates a vicious cycle that escalates and perpetuates the problem. It may be the secondary threat itself which engenders the tendency to self-observe.

Clients look out for 'memory lapses', unusual physical sensations or any other evidence that appears to confirm their worst

Table 2.1   Secondary threats commonly observed in anxiety problems

---

Physical threats
   Heart attack, stroke, tumour, senility, death, injury, etc.

Psychological threats
   Loss of control over mind/emotions/self; e.g. commit suicide, become insane, physically attack someone.

Social threats
   Become an object of ridicule or shame, be rejected, become socially abandoned, etc.

Material threats
   Loss of earnings or other forms of material security.

---

fears. If anything untoward is noticed, clients become more distressed, activation of the autonomic nervous system is increased, with the effect that even greater evidence of, for example, mental illness, loss of control or social embarrassment can be adduced.

Lack of awareness and misinformation
A key to effective counselling is to raise awareness of those aspects of a person's life (memories, conflicts, situations, images, demands and so on) that can be shown to influence the anxiety problem as experienced. Misinformation might also be a factor. Insight is rarely enough. This manual consists of techniques to assist clients to look for alternative explanations of their situation, to attribute to different sources the evidence they produce to justify threat, to change lifestyles, to make specific life decisions, to reduce bodily arousal and to change behaviours.

Failure to confront
A failure to confront the sources of an anxiety problem maintains the problem as it is. A counsellor would not, of course, help a client confront realistic sources of anxiety if the client lacked the resources to mount an effective challenge. The same reasoning occasionally applies to the sources of an anxiety *problem*. A realistic self-appraisal is essential. For instance, a person whose anxiety relates to a fear of leaving a partner should be helped to arrive at an accurate appraisal of his/her reasons for doing so and the likely success of living independently. A counsellor might help a client to reframe the alternatives and develop his/her resources before addressing the anxiety problem more directly.

A client may have coped with an anxiety problem by using psychotropic drugs, alcohol or other substances. Self-medication does not allow a full confrontation with the source of anxiety and so it is generally an obstacle to counselling (see chapter 9). Nevertheless medication may, at times, assist confrontation by helping the client break through a barrier of timidity.

A failure to confront may be encouraged, often unwittingly, by others. Moreover, a client might derive some satisfaction from the attention and extra support that an anxiety problem elicits. Partners or family members might wish to confirm a client's dependent and avoidant behaviour. It is only through careful observation and enquiry that these patterns of interaction can be unearthed.

Clients who withdraw socially or give up activities because of an anxiety problem are liable to depressed mood. Some clients feel stigmatized by the labels they have acquired in their career as patients or have had foisted upon them by their associates. The self-esteem of a client may have been lowered in these ways. Failure to confront may therefore represent a lack of interest, hopelessness or social withdrawal. In this instance, it is all the more important to educate the client about the nature of the problem and to demonstrate, in small ways at first, that change is possible.

Client's focus on the self
The client's distress may become such an all-enveloping concern that he/she dwells persistently on 'symptoms', unwilling to face up to other difficulties, believing this to be impossible while they are 'so anxious'. A large proportion of a client's mental life may be taken up with worry, intrusive thoughts or attention to bodily sensations. Apart from the interference these unwanted intrusions cause, it has been observed that the more anxious a person becomes, the more that attention becomes narrowly focused on potential threats. Pleasant thoughts and diversionary activities tend to get excluded. Thinking develops a rigid, unspontaneous character.

In part, this is due to the fact that clients become hypervigilant for signs of potential threat (in the form of 'odd sensations' or signs of 'mental illness'). Clients may need to be encouraged to develop a more outer-directed focus of attention and to release the grip of their own self-scrutiny.

Absence of satisfying alternatives
A life organized around the avoidance of threat is at least organized. In fact, a source of threat may be so successfully

avoided that it rarely interferes with a person's life. A change of circumstances (being required to fly abroad, speak to an audience, care for a baby) may be the trigger that leads a person to seek help. Avoidance can be sustained tolerably if other life satisfactions are consistent with it. For instance, the point at which a child attends school may be crucial for a mother who is afraid of being alone. The child's presence has, until this time, offset the fear and provided a focus of activity during the day. With the child at school, the mother is alone and (unless she has planned otherwise) is more likely to turn attention to her fears in the absence of the distractions provided by the child. Similarly, later on, when a parent has raised a family or retirement approaches, a lack of outside interests may allow avoidance to spread and dominate a person's life. The problem is acute for clients who have lived with a fear of public places for perhaps twenty years, and then, through bereavement, have had to face independence. In such cases, a counsellor might assist the client to develop his/her personal and material resources and to undertake new interests and roles. In practice this means identifying interests and talents, and suggesting ways of developing social contacts (for example through self-help groups or educational opportunities).

Instrumental factors
As noted above, the expression of an anxiety problem can serve to elicit the attention and sympathy of others. Partners or family members may be drawn in to bolster a client's sense of safety and security, to provide reassurance about potential threats, or help out in practical ways such as shopping.

However, it is a little too easy for the counsellor to use this kind of explanation to account for a lack of progress in counselling. It is best reserved for clients who clearly resist therapeutic interventions aimed at expanding their repertoire. Once resistance of this sort is identified, the focus of counselling can shift accordingly.

Long-term vicious cycles
The long-term repercussions of an anxiety problem may include avoidance of social, work and leisure activities; stigmatizing effects of having an identified problem; demoralizing effects of being incapable of carrying out previously enjoyed activities, use of alcohol, tranquillizers or other drugs to cope with the problem with attendant social consequences; and depressed mood resulting from loss of life satisfactions or hopelessness about the future. Increased activation of the sympathetic nervous system and/or muscular tension may bring about difficulties in relaxing or sleeping,

interference with digestion, sexual arousal and other bodily functions.

It is easy to imagine how these effects of an anxiety problem can exacerbate, in a circular fashion, the original problem. The point will become evident in subsequent case examples.

3

Overview of an Eclectic Approach

This manual sets out the knowledge and skills which can assist the counsellor to work with a client whose presenting anxiety problem is *severe*. Severity is indicated when the problem has resisted commonsense analysis and reasonable attempts to overcome it, and has begun to handicap a person and diminish his/her quality of life. The manual supplements the set of helping strategies with which counsellors are already familiar.

The conceptual framework described earlier stressed that anxiety problems are multifaceted, each facet calling for a sensitive and appropriate counselling response. The optimal style incorporates directive as well as non-directive methods. Some interventions bring the client face to face with the source of anxiety and distress the client. This may feel uncomfortable for counsellors unfamiliar with this approach. Any doubts about using confrontational methods of this kind are usually dispelled by the obvious and rapid benefit they confer on clients. Moreover, discomfort to the client can be minimized by good planning of the session. Generally speaking, clients are highly motivated to overcome their distress, and although the degree of success varies with the type of anxiety problem, the likelihood of benefit is very high.

To work eclectically in this context means recognizing the many and devious routes through which an anxiety problem can develop and be maintained. The surest route through this maze is provided by principles of analysis and observation which, in turn, are likely to suggest a practical solution. The approach selected may not be a textbook example of an 'anxiety management technique'. In fact, to be eclectic in this context should not mean the administration of one technique after another until something 'works'.

I will attempt to specify principles of assessment and intervention in an abstract form so they can be applied flexibly. Whenever possible during counselling, methods are introduced in such a way that feedback can be gained about their effectiveness. The chosen intervention might have to be changed, but the basis for modification should be reasoned speculation rather than trial and error.

The principles described in this manual are cogniti
in nature. It is probably fair to say that counsellor.
sympathetic to this conceptual approach, or do not u.
are unlikely to be able to employ it effectively. This wo
of any approach. It is essential, too, that clients under.
accept the rationale of the counselling interventions ι   ωre
offered. My advocacy of an eclectic approach does not extend to
recommending that different counsellors or therapists work with a
client at the same time. Even pharmacological treatments should
always be undertaken in collaboration with the prescriber (or, at
the least, with a clear undertaking from the client to consult with
the counsellor about any increase, decrease, change or termination
of drug therapy). The decision to refer the client for alternative
forms of help is always open to the counsellor, and this decision
may be taken collaboratively with the client before or after a
cognitive-behavioural intervention.

Manner of working with the client

Cognitive-behavioural counselling is a collaborative, problem-
solving style of working with the client who is:

- helped to identify the main problems (together with their
  antecedents and consequences);
- helped to understand them as examples of learned behaviour;
- engaged in a process of relearning through discussion, experien-
  tial exercises and homework assignments.

Client and counsellor collaborate on the basis of:

- mutual respect;
- an attempt to agree on overall aims; and
- sharing a practical, re-educational model.

Some part of the first session is devoted to establishing this foun-
dation explicitly. Reading material can be supplied to inform the
client about what is on offer and how counselling is likely to
proceed (see Appendix A). The seeds of future failure and
misunderstanding are often sown at this initial stage of 'pre-
counselling', if it is not performed adequately.

Information provided by the client (through self-report or
diaries) is combined with the counsellor's observations and then is
analysed in an attempt to solve the client's problems. Just as the
counsellor provides an objective perspective on the client's

oblems, so the client distances him/herself from the anxiety problem by regarding distress as a problem for critical analysis, capable of being solved. The client might understand his/her problem in the light of a medical theory, a personal philosophy, or a psychodynamic model. It is essential to establish early on that the client is open to a cognitive-behavioural approach, and can reconcile the counsellor's interventions with his/her own account of the problem and personal values.

Clients who are convinced that they have an organic disorder are unlikely to seek counselling. Nevertheless, it cannot be assumed that a client who is initially open to the approach offered will adopt it without resistance, or without proof of effectiveness. It is best to assume that the interpretation of the 'problem' is a subject continually on the agenda and up for renegotiation.

Most clients have several interrelated problems and so different types of intervention may be required. A component of the assessment (see chapter 5) is to establish the relative importance of the problems and to link their respective interventions both practically and theoretically. In practice, the counsellor is continually reassessing the client while intervening. This is inevitable given that problems emerge in a dynamic, changing context.

Characteristics of anxious clients and the nature of the contract

Difficulties experienced with this group of clients are likely to reflect the nature of anxiety itself, for instance that clients have a need both to *contain* and *express* their worries, a *desire* to be reassured and a *resistance* to reassurance, an *impatience* for quick results and a *reluctance* to confront unpleasant situations. It is, perhaps, inevitable that the counsellor is perceived as someone who relieves part of the burden of the problem through reassurance and support. This has certain implications for the counsellor's style of working. People who have anxiety problems are commonly characterized as dependent individuals who seek the support of others when stressed. According to this view, strict boundaries should be enforced with time-limited contracts to ensure that the counsellor does not end up as a permanent bulwark against the client's threatening world, finding him/herself on the end of a telephone line day and night. It is not my experience that this characterization or its implications are valid (although this scenario could be enacted if a counsellor unwittingly plays the role of comforter).

One effective style of working embodies a disciplined form of relationship allowing a client to maximally use the counsellor as a source of safety (and reassurance about the ultimate outcome), while minimally permitting the client to receive any reassurance or encouragement concerning exaggerated threats, diversionary (i.e. ungrounded) somatic complaints, or the 'necessity' of avoidance. The counsellor models the attitude that a calm, deliberate and dogged approach will produce results, which in virtually all cases it does. As the client begins to trust the counsellor, more rapid confrontational techniques may be employed. The style can be summarized as follows.

An open-ended contract

This sort of contract is conditional on both parties agreeing that some progress is being made. An initial arrangement might be to review after 3–5 sessions to ensure that progress is possible. An open-ended contract reduces a client's concern that they will be left in a worse state after being encouraged to face up to fears (this concern is realistic and may be based on previous failed therapeutic encounters). It also lessens the sense of entrapment produced by a short-term contract which exerts pressure to succeed by a certain date. Entrapment by constraints of this kind is almost universally disliked by anxious people. Lastly, it acknowledges that progress may take a long time and may require considerable persistence.

In my experience, clients offered open-ended, though conditional, contracts do not become overly dependent. Sessions may be frequent at first (up to several times per week), but quickly reduced in frequency to weekly, biweekly, and later on still, every 3–6 weeks. Clients often appreciate the availability of a counsellor (to receive a telephone call or arrange an unscheduled session) even though the offer is rarely, or never, taken up.

In most instances, counselling is complete within 5–20 sessions. However, some clients may continue to make progress over 3–4 years while the total number of sessions received remains relatively low. Length of the session varies according to the technique employed and often deviates from the conventional one hour. The spacing of sessions reflects the emphasis on self-managed task assignments and prescriptive strategies in cognitive-behavioural counselling.

When the client is facing up to distressing experiences, it is clearly not in the client's interest to drag out this phase of counselling for too long. Typically, the anxious client does not dread a session in which a threat is confronted. The session is planned to give a client a sense of mastery. It is not unusual for the client to leave feeling elated.

To empathize but never sympathize

To empathize is to show by careful questioning and reflection that the client's thoughts and feelings are clearly understood. Few clients welcome sympathy (that is, condolences), but some anxious people respond to it, by elaborating on their 'symptoms'. When empathizing, a counsellor may feel that he or she is giving undue credence to improbable future imaginary events leading to an impulse to step in, reassure or discount the evidence. The important point here is that empathy is essential to allow the client freedom to share shameful, distressing or seemingly ridiculous notions. Rather than being drawn into countering such ideas, the counsellor should be content, initially, to draw them out, perhaps suggesting even worse scenarios that the client can strongly disavow.

However, even an empathic response can lead to unproductive counselling. A client who expresses many worries as somatic preoccupations may trap the counsellor into circular and frustrating discussions about the validity or likelihood of various hypothetical situations. In extreme cases, effective work is precluded. One strategy to overcome this problem is to point out what is happening and contract to talk only about agreed topics. If the client fails to comply, the counsellor may, after pointing this out, simply say nothing until the client returns to an agreed agenda. Advocacy of this tactic should not be taken to imply that the client's worries or somatic concerns are irrelevant; they may indeed be the focus of the intervention.

To tolerate irregular progress and setbacks

An anxiety problem can fluctuate considerably over time. What a client can achieve on one day may become impossible the next. Clients should be informed about this variability and be led to expect it. The vicious cycles so commonly observed in anxiety problems may be fed by the client's negative evaluation of his/her own performance or by the counsellor's inadequately hidden disapproval when homework assignments are not fulfilled. In reviewing progress, it is important to highlight achievements and to take a long-term perspective. The causes for lack of success should be carefully analysed as an opportunity to gain constructive information. Responsibility for lack of progress should rest, as a matter of course, with the counsellor. Thus, if the client's motivation to pursue counselling or to work on the lines agreed is in question, it is the counsellor's responsibility to regard this issue as the first priority. Intolerance of a client's activities should be limited to anything that clearly undermines the aims of counselling. The client may be unaware that the action is undermining, in which case the reason can be offered for discussion. Examples might be failure to disclose important information, changing or stopping medication without consultation, or arriving drunk to sessions. Many of the contractual conditions under which counselling is offered will have been made explicit in the pre-counselling phase.

To involve others where appropriate
Partners, friends, members of the family or others may become involved in the counselling for one of the following reasons:

- for the counsellor to obtain their perspective on the client, and to seek information;
- to inform them about aims and procedures when interventions impinge on their lives in some way;
- to seek collaboration, for example, in helping a client face up to, rather than avoid, certain situations;
- to ensure, at least, non-interference with interventions if a more positive attitude is not forthcoming;
- to reassure and educate someone who may be unwittingly contributing to an anxiety problem;
- to gain the services of a helper or volunteer on a more permanently arranged or formal basis.

It can be helpful for people closely involved with a client to be supplied with reading matter which informs them about anxiety problems and the sort of techniques employed to overcome them (see Appendix A).

Counselling anxiety problems – general aims

The general aims follow from the conceptual model developed in chapter 1. Anxiety problems may involve complex chains of behaviour and vicious cycle phenomena. Thought, action and physiological reactions are all likely to play a part. For this reason, while the general aims are unvarying, the methods employed can be quite dissimilar.

First aim – encouraging the client to adopt a reflective problem-solving set

This aim must be fulfilled before anything useful can be achieved with the methods described in this manual. The methods themselves carry an implicit message which reinforces the counsellor's rationale. Before undertaking any intervention (even asking the client to monitor a problem in a diary), its purpose should have been explained to the client's satisfaction. Apart from a lack of knowledge of the psychology of fear and stress, which is fairly easily remedied, there are two obstacles to a problem-solving attitude that commonly present themselves. The first is a client's belief that his/her mental and physical discomfort is caused by a medical disorder. The second is the use of drugs or alcohol to suppress an anxiety problem.

Second aim – modification of exaggerated or improbable threat

Unrealistic appraisal of threat is a core feature of anxiety problems. It should be distinguished from timidity or 'faint-heartedness', which can be defined as an extreme intolerance of the discomfort experienced when facing the normal challenges of life. Unrealistic appraisals may be based on:

- false information;
- exaggerated estimates of the likelihood or magnitude of threatening events;
- low estimates of the client's own ability to cope by countering the threat.

Unrealistic threat can be modified directly by cognitive and behavioural methods and, possibly indirectly, through interventions that raise morale generally. Cognitive techniques strengthen a client's ability to reason logically and in more optimistic ways. Behavioural methods, involving confrontation, lead to a re-appraisal of threat when the consequences of facing up to it are found to be less harmful than anticipated.

Third aim – increased confidence and improved adjustment

Anxiety is rarely an isolated problem unrelated to a client's overall adjustment to life. A phobia that is elicited by circumscribed situations (such as snakes) may represent an exception to this rule, but even here the phobic problem will have disrupted the person's life and probably led to a loss of self-esteem. Once the client has overcome the problem, confidence and a feeling of well-being are likely to return.

In some clients, low self-esteem and other psychological

difficulties contribute to the origin of anxiety problems rather than reflect their consequences. If we accept that anxiety is the obverse of security/safety/confidence, then addressing ourselves to the latter is just as important as eliminating the former. Clients commonly have difficulty in three main areas:

- intimate and other interpersonal relationships;
- problems of chronic stress, related either to genuine burdens or lack of skill in managing stressors;
- inability to resolve the effects of past traumas.

Counselling for anxiety problems cannot be divorced from counselling in all the areas just mentioned. Case examples will be used to illustrate this point.

Fourth aim – developing the client's problem-solving strategies

Anxiety may result from a general difficulty in coping with day-to-day problems. For this group of clients, help in overcoming a specific problem may be short lived. New challenges and stressors are likely to re-evoke an anxious response. This 'anxiety-proneness' may be related to unassertiveness, fear of failure, low self-esteem, over conscientiousness, or other behavioural dispositions. The aim of the counsellor is to teach general problem-solving strategies, applying them to the concrete day-to-day difficulties that arise. In time, through repeatedly dealing successfully with concrete problems, the client learns how to apply a strategy without the assistance of the counsellor. In other words, the strategy is internalized.

4

Formulation of Anxiety Problems

Formulating a client's problem is a prelude to intervening. In practice, the process continues throughout counselling. Exploring the reasons why an intervention fails may provide one with a better formulation and a new intervention. An intervention should be derived in a purposeful way from the formulation, that is, based on a psychological hypothesis about the factors causing or maintaining the problem.

In formulating a problem, a counsellor attempts to make sense of it by drawing on a general principle or empirical generalization. Cognitive-behavioural formulations have diverse roots in theory, and the field has now broadened out so much that it is difficult to specify the conceptual model precisely. Be that as it may, the formulation can draw upon any relevant research findings.

Cognitive-behavioural counsellors are pragmatic, and so theoretical rationales have been justified by the success of the techniques associated with them. The commitment to scientific evaluation and a self-critical attitude has generally ensured that progress has been made in understanding why the techniques work. Some theoretical ideas have been given up and new ones have been acquired. Some of the core theoretical concepts are discussed below.

In practice, the formulation can be quite simple, specifying the main problems and what sort of events elicit and maintain them. Maintenance refers to the process by which the events following the expression of the problem serve to reinforce and hold it in its present form. The maintaining event might be a smile of approval or the 'relief' of removing an unpleasant state of affairs. A client should be encouraged to observe what events precede and follow the problem behaviour, and the formulation, as it develops, can be phrased in terms of what it is that heightens or lessens distress. Knowing what the relevant events are (including thoughts he or she may be having) gives the client an opportunity to predict and control distress. The therapeutic effect of simply naming and listing problems should not be underestimated.

A counsellor should aim to share a formulation, but how this is done depends partly on the level of sophistication of the client. A counsellor might entertain hypotheses and formulations that are not shared, either because the client would not, at the time, understand them or would obviously reject them. The aim, however, is to collaborate openly, using as the baseline and springboard the client's own understanding of the problem.

A formulation might include the influence of events, past or present, that cannot be changed. Nevertheless, these should be conceptualized because an intervention is always a compromise between the ideal and the attainable. For example, a client may come to realize that certain problems, as he or she formulates them, are insoluble. One of the goals of counselling might be to assist the client to accept this, and to generate feasible alternatives.

The formulation influences what goals are set and in what order they are tackled. The first step is to describe the problems in behavioural and cognitive terms, and to carry out a functional analysis.

Behavioural description and functional analysis

From behavioural therapy has come the stress on describing behaviour in its environmental context, and doing so in rather concrete and specific terms. Human acts in real situations cannot, of course, be described with the same objective precision as the lever-pressing responses of rats in Skinner boxes – nor is this the aim of behavioural description. The purpose instead is to use plain descriptive language which makes as few inferences as possible about motive or global personality characteristics. The observation 'Bill looked in the mirror' implies less than 'Bill admired himself in the mirror'. Both may be true, but the latter excludes other interpretations such as Bill was looking at a spot, Bill noticed that he had forgotten to shave, and so on. The relationship with the environment is different in each case. We would need to study Bill's looking at himself in the mirror as part of a stream of behaviour, that is in relation to other antecedent and consequent events. Relating events together is known as functional analysis. For example, if Bill headed for the bathroom and began shaving, we might feel more confident that Bill's glance in the mirror did act as a prompt (or *discriminative stimulus*) for shaving, and was not a form of self-admiration. The act of checking in the mirror is reinforced on the occasions that shaving proves necessary. (What maintains shaving would require further analysis.)

The breakdown of the stream of behaviour into antecedent – behaviour – consequence (ABC) is a very flexible schema, in which, for example, the consequence of one behaviour might be the antecedent for the next. Some behaviourists regard thoughts as sub-vocal speech and the thought is conceived as playing the roles of both response and stimulus. Physiological responses of the body also enter into the chain, first because they accompany human actions, and second because they produce internal stimuli such as the sensations associated with a rapid pulse, tight muscles or full bladder.

The sequence of ABCs can be interpreted as a causal chain when it can be shown that the presence, absence, timing or frequency of one element is dependent on the presence of another. To take a simple example: a client becomes anxious in the presence of spiders but not beetles, butterflies or ants. Spiders are a causal stimulus antecedent to anxious behaviour. Pursuing this example further: running away from spiders is followed by the consequence of 'spider-absent'. The absence of this stimulus can be viewed as the causally effective event that maintains running away. We can infer this because if running away did not lead to the absence of spiders (spiders were inescapable), we would expect some new behaviour to emerge such as fighting spiders or freezing on the spot. In learning theory terms, 'running away' would undergo *extinction*. This is the process that occurs when the effective event for maintaining a behaviour is removed. The range of behaviours that a person is able to call forth in a given situation is referred to as the *behavioural repertoire*. So in this case when running away is extinguished, or suppressed in some other way, two other responses in the repertoire, freezing or fighting, appear in its stead.

In anxiety problems, the events that are causally effective in maintaining anxious behaviours often turn out to be highly unpleasant stimulus events or situations, real or imagined. For instance, the sight of the spider might suggest a further sequence of events in which the spider crawls over the person and bites them. So far, we have talked of the causal chain of events as 'out there' in the real world. When we talk of *imagined* events, we bring in the concept of a person's internal representation of the outside world. This is the *cognitive* element that we will return to in a moment. How a person imagines things to be is often how they think things *really* are, but sometimes a person recognizes that their representation of events is inaccurate (but still compelling).

To return to our example: a spider phobic might regard spiders as harmless, but remain unable to stop themselves acting towards them as dangerous and having frightening thoughts about them, such as the improbable idea that spiders bite. In many cases it is the imagined sequence (*symbolic representation*) of events that is paramount in determining action. This symbolic or cognitive aspect of behaviour may become as automatic and habitual as the response of running away.

Counselling can be thought of as a process promoting *relearning*. The way in which a person thinks about themselves, or a situation, can be influenced by verbal means (for example through information about the sequence of events in the 'real' world, different interpretation of events, persuasive discourse), or through behavioural means. A person can be *instructed* to behave differently (sometimes called a 'behavioural experiment') or *encouraged/induced* to behave differently. In the former case, the purpose is to show the client that reality differs from the way they conceive it to be and, thereby, to change their idea of it. In the latter case, a person learns not only to think differently, but in addition may learn to respond more adaptively (this may depend on additional advice, modelling or training of adaptive responses).

Information on its own – for instance being told that spiders don't bite – is rarely effective in producing change. Information acquired through experience is generally more powerful. Discovering through experience that spiders are harmless and friendly creatures generally leads to a permanent loss of fear. The processes that underlie behavioural methods may not be very different from those taking place in cognitive methods. However, knowledge of the world (such that X leads to Y, or doing A produces B) may not be readily put into words or images and, for this reason, verbal techniques may be ineffective in producing change.

A behavioural and functional analysis simply makes assumptions about what events are causally important. This then suggests interventions to change their relationship. Let us first consider a classification of behavioural relationships between events before going on to discuss cognitive terminology.

When consequent events are divided up into those that are 'positive' and 'negative', the number of different types of causally effective arrangements is quite small. These arrangements or *learning paradigms* have been deliberately created and studied in the laboratory (see Table 4.1), to find out about their characteristic effects. Of course, it is not immediately obvious from an ABC analysis what arrangements best describe the state of affairs. This is one of the arts of cognitive-behavioural therapy. For example, does an infant's cry on being put to bed relate to the consequence of being placed in darkness (consequent 1), or, the departure of the parent (consequent 2)? The choice will suggest which learning paradigm is appropriate, and may determine the intervention that is selected. Correct analysis, aided by further observation of, and

Table 4.1   *Learning paradigms*

Paradigm sequence of events	Names	Example	Effect
Response followed by positive consequence	Reward learning Positive reinforcement	Approval for task done	Response (performance of task) increases in frequency
Response followed by absence of (expected) positive consequence	Extinction Frustrative non-reward	Lack of expected approval for task done	Response (performance of task) decreases in frequency
Response followed by removal of positive consequence (unexpected)	Response cost Time-out	Parking fine for parking illegally	Response (parking illegally) decreases in frequency
Response followed by negative consequence	Punishment Passive avoidance	Being ignored when starting conversation	Response (starting conversation) decreases in frequency
Response removes negative consequence	Escape learning	Fleeing from phobic situation	Response (fleeing from phobic situation) increases in frequency
Response followed by removal of (expected) negative consequence	Negative reinforcement Active avoidance	Avoidance of phobic situation	Response (not entering phobic situation) increases in frequency

experimentation with, key events is crucial to success.

This introduction to behavioural theory has been very brief, and the reader is referred to source books for further information.

Cognitive analysis

Cognitive analysis attends to the way clients symbolically represent their world and their own place in it. It locates the cause for anxiety problems in unhelpful or even irrational ways of thinking. Unlike behavioural analysis which emphasizes environmental determinants of a problem, it looks upon events in the world as *sources of evidence* for or against a person's way of thinking.

The process of representing the world and of operating with those representations is, in part, unconscious. We are not necessarily aware of the interpretations we place on events. Nevertheless, we can articulate chains of thoughts, state our beliefs and use metaphor or imagery to describe and capture the essence of the way we think and feel. In cognitive analysis, these conscious expressions of our thinking are referred to as surface thoughts, in order to contrast them with *core beliefs* or *underlying assumptions*. The latter can be compared to rules, summarizing in a more general way the basis of our thinking. Core beliefs are less accessible but more important, because they underpin our surface thoughts in a large number of situations. Certain core beliefs are inflexible and create difficulties for the person who holds them. Clients who think in this way can be helped to articulate the core beliefs that underlie their surface thoughts and to dispute them.

In anxious clients, surface thinking in anxiety-provoking situations may take the following form: 'I must be seriously ill'; 'If this carries on I won't be able to stand it'; 'What if the 'plane crashes'; 'She must be thinking I'm stupid', 'Everybody is looking at me', and so on. These thoughts can be examined further by finding out how they are chained to other thoughts, and to more general assumptions about the world. In this way, certain negative core beliefs may be unearthed. For example, the core belief 'I am unable to cope on my own' might underlie a surface fear of the death of a spouse. Cognitive therapists contend that holding negative and unhelpful beliefs of this kind is a primary cause of anxiety problems and of the associated unpleasant sensations and defensive behaviours. Change the thinking and the problem should go.

In a limited way, we know this to be true. If a plane crashes and we believe a friend is on the flight, our distress will be great; if the belief proves to be mistaken, our distress is relieved immediately. However, cognitive techniques do not rely merely on correcting mistaken beliefs. Unrealistic thinking is entrenched and maintained despite contrary evidence. More powerful means have been devised to dispute it. One technique is behavioural – tasks are devised to show the client that the world is not the way it is conceived to be. Another relies on verbal disputation, a process of questioning in which the client provides evidence to support the way they think. These methods, which will be illustrated later, dispute (1) false or unhelpful beliefs; (2) extreme (absolute) evaluations; (3) certain styles of thinking, for example ignoring evidence that doesn't fit a certain view of the world, or seeing things in black and white terms instead of shades of grey.

The surface thinking of anxious clients commonly takes the form of a chain of ever more threatening interpretations of events, culminating in an image of something quite catastrophic. Threatening interpretations give rise to physiological changes and to behaviours that may provide further evidence for the threat, or even grounds for a new threat. In this way a vicious spiral is created. The elements in the chain can be extremely variable from one client to another. The elements may include sensations, feelings or other qualities of experience, behaviour and its effects, and interpretations already made. The elements may be events that are happening to the self, or refer to the thoughts/behaviours of other persons. The elements are linked together by *inferences* (logical steps which relate one element to the next) or *evaluations* ('this is bad, awful, terrible, etc.').

For instance, the thought 'I can't cope with anxiety' might lead to the thought 'I ought to be able to cope' (evaluation), on to 'I must be a worthless person' (inference that if I cannot cope, I must be worthless). This sort of chaining, which involves increasingly catastrophic events or damning self-evaluations, is critical in some anxiety problems. The introduction of cognitive techniques has led to significant progress in effective counselling in this area.

Anxious thinking may occur only when the client is in certain situations or in a worried/low mood. Consequently, cognitive techniques may be more effective when the client has already been made anxious. This can be achieved through the use of evocative imagery, or simply by introducing the client to fearful situations. The counsellor encourages the client to dispute negative or unhelpful thoughts, while he/she is having them. The process of uncovering chains of unrealistic thinking requires great sensitivity, especially when clients regard their thoughts as ridiculous, shameful or disgusting. Examples of cognitive analysis are given in chapters 7 and 8.

Case example to illustrate behavioural and cognitive analysis

Background information   A 35-year-old male is living in rented accommodation with his elderly father who is said to be depressed. His mother died six months earlier. He has lived with his parents since the break-up of his marriage at the age of 30. He has no educational qualifications and has worked at a number of unskilled and semi-skilled jobs since the age of 15. He is currently unemployed. His leisure interests are social drinking, playing pool and going to night clubs. He has a number of long-standing friends, but finds that he generally has to make the initial contacts for a meeting.

Reason for referral The referring psychiatrist mentioned panic episodes as well as difficulties in relationships with women. The client complains primarily of 'tension' and 'depression'. He describes choking while eating three years earlier when he 'panicked'. He fears now that he cannot swallow without choking and avoids eating in public places. He says he lacks confidence and is unable to work because of his 'tension'.

History of complaints and associated professional contacts

Age 25: Sought help from his GP for 'nerves'.
Age 29: Again sought help, feeling that he was a 'hopeless case', 'worthless' and 'pessimistic'. He turned down an offer of group therapy.
Age 32: Investigated for physical symptoms at an ear, nose and throat hospital, with negative results. Obtained weekly counselling for several months.
Age 33: Offered group therapy but attended only on a few occasions. Saw himself as needing medical not psychotherapeutic treatment. Continued to receive psychiatric support for two years.

Over the last ten years he has received various minor tranquillizers. He disliked the side-effects of anti-depressant medication and stopped taking it. He is not generally in favour of taking drugs but finds tranquillizers helpful in calming him down.

General History He was brought up in a tough neighbourhood and received some taunting from his peers. He was very attached to his mother who was a lively, warm but domineering woman. He now feels guilty about 'the problems he caused her'. He describes his father as a passive man who did not exert sufficient control over him. He does not currently respect his father. He says he was a shy youth with few girlfriends. At the age of 27, he married someone he had known for three years. Divorce followed three years later. Currently he does not report any sexual difficulties, but he does feel anxious and inadequate in the presence of a woman whom he sees as a potential future partner.

History of anxiety complaints As a child he had strong fears of the dark, and feared death as a teenager. His first visit to a GP, on account of 'nerves' was prompted by an experience of his head feeling 'funny and empty'. He developed a fear of driving in heavy traffic but overcame this himself. At the age of 32 he developed several somatic symptoms including a feeling that 'his breath was going' especially while driving. A year later he choked on some food and 'could not get his breath for thirty seconds'. Subsequently, he found he could not swallow liquids or food with ease, and he also choked on a second occasion.

Depressed mood He describes his personality as basically happy-go-lucky with no marked swings of mood. Currently, his mood is quite variable and he has an occasional suicidal thought. He experiences self-blame and also sees himself as worthless. Although he says he is depressed 'most of the time', his sleep, appetite and sexual desire are not obviously affected. He is grieving his mother's death and still avoids talking about her, or visiting places with which she is associated.

Comment Before going on to consider current behavioural problems, some initial conclusions can be drawn. It would be misleading to give the impression that the information supplied above was obtained in one interview, or in anything like the order it is presented. Placing the material in this order helps us to conceptualize his problems. At this point we can state the following:

1 In common with many clients, his anxiety complaints are embedded in other problems, e.g. difficulty in relationships with women, mourning his mother's recent death, recent divorce, and unemployment.
2 The anxiety problems, nevertheless, have their own history, apparently precipitated by an anomalous perception (head feels 'funny and empty'), and later by 'choking'. His childhood fears suggest an anxious disposition.
3 He has a medical orientation to his complaints, and generally does not see how his 'symptoms' relate to his life history or lifestyle.
4 There is evidence that he finds it difficult to solve day-to-day problems. It isn't easy for him to control his impulses, and he admits that he has been 'living in a fantasy world'.

Counselling could, and did, focus on problems unrelated to the more obvious complaints of tension and somatic symptoms. It was decided, however, to give the anxiety problem top priority because it was clearly interfering in a direct way with his life, for example his ability to work or to socialize. So the assessment that follows concentrates on this aspect.

Behavioural and cognitive analysis of current problems
The information for this analysis was derived from interview analysis of recent episodes of distress recorded in a diary, and observation of behaviour in critical situations. The purpose was to identify:

1 the behaviours/thoughts/feelings that are unwanted and problematic;
2 the behaviours/thoughts/feelings whose *absence* is problematic;
3 the stimulus antecedents and consequents for the above;
4 the surface thinking and core beliefs that are associated with (1) and (2);
5 general styles of coping with problems that are creating difficulty for the client.

Problems were identified as follows:

Unpleasant mood Described as tension, anxiety and restlessness, this was associated with various thoughts about himself. (I'm a failure, no good, a psychiatric case, expecting a rebuff, putting on a front, are my friends my enemies? I've treated my mother badly.) It was difficult to establish stimulus antecedents for these negative self-reflections, but it was evident that they increased when he was encouraged to think about the concrete problems he was facing (relationships, work, etc.). The most obvious consequents of his negative self-focus were the use of tranquillizers and the absence of constructive problem-solving activities.

Somatic sensations For example, breathlessness, tightness in the chest and muscular tension. Our client reported that worrying bodily sensations could occur at any time as well as in more anxiety-provoking situations. They appeared to increase in frequency in the presence of a sympathetic listener. With professionals he sought reassurance about their diagnostic implications, but when reassurance was provided, its effect was short-lived.

Inability to eat in public This problem dated from the 'choking' episode. The following information was obtained at interview. The client

- is able to eat at home with family, or in private, anywhere, without difficulty;
- avoids eating in the presence of others, male or female, but eating in a crowded restaurant (especially at some distance from the exit) would be more difficult than a snack bar, which in turn would be more difficult than a snack in a friend's house;
- shows fear that others would look at him if he choked, and this would be embarrassing, especially if he felt the urge to escape quickly from a restaurant (e.g. without paying);
- is afraid that he might choke and die;
- has almost as much difficulty swallowing liquids as foods.

It was decided to assess the problem further by observing him eat in a snack bar. He agreed to be accompanied and drink a cup of tea sitting on a stool close to the exit. Here he was asked about his thoughts/feelings while clearly in an anxious frame of mind. Direct observation confirmed the severity of his problem, and the content of his negative thoughts. Later observations, while eating in a café), also revealed the rapid speed with which he ate. On questioning him, it was discovered that his family had rarely eaten together at a table. It was customary for him to eat in a semi-lying position while watching television. His rapid eating was consistent with his quick, nervous movements, chain smoking, and rapid speech in many situations.

Formulation
The purpose of the formulation is to develop psychological hypotheses to explain the client's difficulties, taking into account the fact that problems are interlinked, and that some sources of difficulty may be temporary. The value of the formulation for setting goals becomes apparent as we discuss it. The process of defining and negotiating the goals of counselling is separate from the formulation of problems, though the two processes are clearly related. On the one hand, the counsellor is unlikely to agree to setting unattainable, impractical or unethical goals. On the other hand, a client will not be motivated to work towards goals that are not his own. Bearing in mind the formulation and the goals, a set of interventions is agreed and initiated.

At this point, we can consider our client's difficulties in terms of the causal and maintaining factors described earlier (Figure 2.1).

1 Chronic sources of behavioural disorganization Two possible sources have already been mentioned – lack of employment and his failure to develop a long-term relationship with a woman. These two factors contribute to his low self-opinion, which interferes with his ability to adopt a constructive approach to his problems. However, in so far as he cannot eat in public, and, in his view, cannot ask a woman out, or seek certain kinds of employment on this account, these problems might begin to resolve themselves if his fear of eating in public were to be eliminated. Therefore, interventions directed at his lack of employment and intimate relationships were temporarily shelved. In addition, he was grieving his mother's death. As his grief seemed to be appropriate and was lessening (and he did not consider it a problem), it was not felt necessary to make this a central aspect of counselling.

2 Short-term vicious cycles The feared consequences of choking and hurrying to make an exit, can be seen as elements in a short-term vicious spiral. Anxious apprehension of these consequences mediates bodily reactions (e.g. dry mouth, inhibition of swallowing, muscle tension) that exacerbate the eating problem. On entering an eating place, he is likely to focus his attention on his throat, experience a tightening sensation, and fear the worst.

His anticipation of choking is to some degree realistic. Choking, though obviously not death by choking, has occurred before. It is important in designing the intervention to suppress the choking response or circumvent it. Otherwise, experience in some measure confirms his fears. Although the likelihood of his becoming a public spectacle or choking to death appeared to be overestimated, it was judged that these 'catastrophes' were expected only in the eating situation and did not represent, or relate to, underlying dysfunctional assumptions.

3 Lack of awareness and misinformation Our client was not so much misinformed as lacking information about bodily changes associated with anxiety. The role of the autonomic nervous system and vicious cycles in producing bodily sensations were explained, as was the purpose of confrontation and the expected decline in fear with repeated exposure to eating situations.

His belief that he had a 'psychiatric illness' was also explored and an attempt was made to reframe this medical interpretation of his 'symptoms'. His heightened attention to somatic sensations was not based on a clearly articulated notion of illness, but he worried and sought reassurance about any new sensation he experienced. The sensations were explained as normal accompaniments of stress and bodily arousal.

His somatic complaining may also have served as an avoidance response, which relieved him of the distressing prospect of facing real-life difficulties. I have already noted that he saw his 'psychiatric condition' (which included taking tranquillizers) as not only shameful, but also as a reason for failing to engage in constructive solutions to his problems.

4   *Failure to confront*   His avoidance of public eating situations was near total. Thus, his fear of the consequences (embarrassment, choking, dying) was protected from extinction. Avoidance behaviour had generalized rapidly after the first choking incident, and it had been intermittently reinforced by further choking or discomforting episodes. Moreover, he had elaborated several imaginary negative consequences of choking in a public place (for example, imagining having to escape hurriedly from a restaurant without paying the bill, being chased by the proprietor).

5   *Absence of constructive alternatives*   With regard to his avoidance of eating in public, our client could see no constructive way of coping with this except to eat in isolation. He had no suggestions for managing his distress. In a wider sense, he had employment skills, charm, and was socially adroit but his ability to make use of these assets was limited by his avoidance of public eating situations. He also lacked confidence in his ability to maintain an intimate relationship with a woman.

The account he gave of his marriage and current, largely unrealistic, notions of an ideal partner, indicated that his relationship problems would continue unless he was able to modify his expectations and behaviour in this area of his life.

6   *Instrumental factors*   Here we consider whether the expression of his problem enables him to obtain advantages not so far noted. The way in which the anxiety problem enabled him to avoid facing up to other difficulties has already been mentioned. However, his avoidance seemed to result from helplessness rather than from a resistance to change because he would be giving up positive benefits.

7   *Long-term vicious cycles*   One of the longer-term consequences of his anxiety problem was lowered self-esteem. In practical terms, he saw his 'anxiety' as an obstacle to work and relationships. To some degree, his depression may be attributed to a pessimistic view of his future. Therefore, aside from any other problems of adjustment, we may view the anxiety problem as playing a major part in his demoralization. He is unable to find work and new relationships because of his 'anxiety problem' and he is unlikely to solve his

'anxiety problem' without making progress in each of these areas. The operation of a long-term vicious cycle is clearly evident in this case.

Goal Setting

Four interim goals were agreed:

1 to adopt a practical and constructive approach to his problems rather than focus on 'symptoms';
2 to eat in public without anxiety;
3 to provide supportive counselling and advice regarding work, relationship or family matters as the need arose (in preparation for more focused intervention later);
4 to implement a gradual reduction of medication.

It should be noted that the goals do not include the reduction of 'tension' or 'general anxiety'. The reasons for this are that

– it would encourage his symptom focus and medical orientation;
– it was predicted that his dysphoria would be relieved if the first and second goals could be achieved;
– he was judged to be too agitated to follow instructions for, or respond to, body-focused methods such as relaxation training.

Interventions

A broadly behavioural rather than cognitive approach was chosen because it was difficult to get him to reflect in a rational and systematic manner on his problems. Information was provided in a brief didactic form.

First goal A problem-solving approach was taught by

– setting an agenda for a session;
– ignoring reference to symptoms and reminding him of the agenda;
– engaging him in problem-solving tasks within, and between, sessions.

The fulfilment of the second goal, was in fact, a vehicle for demonstrating that problems (such as eating in public) could be broken down into small steps and solved.

Second goal A programme of gradually confronting public eating situations was instituted (see chapter 6). The programme incorporated a number of objectives:

1 prolonged, safe familiarization leading to an extinction of fear;
2 giving our client confidence in his ability to prevent choking;
3 examining and disputing evidence for his belief that he will make a public spectacle of himself or die by choking (in the eating situation).

Our client was asked to consolidate what he had learned in the accompanied sessions by confronting the same situations on his own or with friends (see chapter 7 for guidelines on self-managed programmes). Our client acquired confidence in his ability to prevent choking by following some simple instructions when he first felt any premonition of difficulty in swallowing. He was to

- stop eating or drinking;
- put down his eating utensils;
- not attempt to swallow;
- to sit back and wait until he felt calm and able to continue eating/drinking.

The counsellor identified moments for putting this routine into practice by observing the client. The instructions were prompted by being spoken aloud by the counsellor. After a calm pause, swallowing had always occurred involuntarily. Later, the client followed the routine after the first prompt, and later still he was able to identify when he should initiate it himself.

Public eating situations were dealt with in an ascending order of difficulty, based on a 'hierarchy' worked out in advance (see chapter 6). The client was asked to reveal his thoughts while in these anxiety-provoking situations. Expression of unrealistic threats was handled by

- disputing the evidence for them; for example looking around the café and detecting individuals who noticed his behaviour; producing evidence that they thought he was making a spectacle of himself;
- discerning possible 'escape routes' in the event of his catastrophic scenario materializing; for example imagining his leaving the café in a panic and then waiting outside until he had calmed down and re-entering, or pretending that he had left because he felt sick, in order to avoid the embarrassment of failure to pay his bill.

These alternatives were reassuring and, in reality, never needed to be put into practice.

Third goal Counselling was helpful in so far as a number of situations arose regarding employment possibilities and encounters with women friends. These provided an opportunity to explore his expectations and methods of dealing with these situations. These aspects will not be discussed as they are not directly relevant to the purposes of this manual.

Fourth goal Medication was reduced following the guidelines presented in chapter 9.

Outcome
This client entirely overcame the problem of eating in public over the space of fifteen months, eventually attending a formal works dinner. Counselling sessions were initially weekly for 12 weeks and then spaced out to a frequency of every 4–6 weeks. He found satisfying work over this period, and his general dysphoria and negative self-reflection diminished to an acceptable level without direct intervention.

Suggestions for further reading

The basic principles of behavioural and functional analysis can be found in most textbooks on behavioural or cognitive-behavioural therapy, but see, in relation to anxiety problems, Emmelkamp (1982) and Hawton et al. (1989). On cognitive analysis see Beck et al. (1985), Blackburn and Davidson (1990) and Trower et al. (1988).

5

Assessment of Anxiety Problems

The aim of assessment is to gather sufficient information to formulate the problem(s) and decide on an initial intervention. This aim is normally accomplished in one or two sessions, but if it is not, it is better to prolong the assessment than proceed without a full picture. The counsellor should remain continually on the alert for, and in fact expect, important new information to come to light throughout the therapeutic process. Routine enquiries should be made about topics that could be relevant to the problem, but are not spontaneously mentioned.

This chapter will describe methods for systematic collection of information. As a formulation takes shape, information gathering is increasingly guided by hypothesis-testing.

Methods of assessment

The principal methods of assessment are:

1 the interview (of client and significant others);
2 behavioural observation (in simulated or real situations);
3 self-observation (e.g. diary recording of distressing events);
4 checklists and questionnaires;
5 exploration in fantasy of problem themes.

The use of these methods will be discussed in relation to the objectives of assessment. This chapter will concentrate on *assessing* anxiety problems, assuming that counsellors already possess the skills to establish rapport, identify problems apart from anxiety, and adjust their interviewing style to the characteristics of the client.

First assessment interview(s)

The objectives of the initial assessment are as follows:

Table 5.1 *Checklist of common fears and anxieties*

Animal fears	*Public places*
Snakes	Walking in the street
Spiders	Shops
Dogs	Travelling by underground train
Cats	Travelling by bus
Birds	Travelling by car
Bees or wasps	Flying
Rats or mice	Cinema or theatre
	Bridges
Social fears	High places
Speaking in front of an audience	Deep water
Meeting someone in authority	Lifts
Meeting someone of the opposite sex	Having hair cut
Having an argument	
Being criticized	*Illness, injury, disease*
Being observed by others	Attending hospital
Going to a party	Sight of blood
Making a mistake	Having an injection
Looking foolish	Sharp objects
Hearing loud, angry voices	Going to the dentist
	Doctors
Miscellaneous	Heart stopping
Darkness	Being mentally ill
Thunder and lightning	Surgical operation
Being left alone	Germs
Using public toilets	Thought of dying
Signing your name in front of others	Fainting
	Vomiting or seeing others vomit
	Suffocation

1 to elicit a brief account of the main problem(s) and their current impact, ensuring coverage rather than depth, at this point. The purpose here is to obtain an initial thumbnail sketch of the problems before going into detail;

2 to gather background information such as age, marital status, living arrangements, family of origin, religious/ethnic identity, occupation, educational history, social and leisure interests;

3 to obtain a history of the main problems and associated life events and existential circumstances;

4 to obtain a brief history of medical and psychiatric treatment (if any) and note current medications, especially psychotropic drugs and their prescribed doses. A history of depression and current mood state should be included here;

5 to assess the client's response to previous therapy/treatments/

Table 5.2 *Sensations and feelings commonly experienced in anxiety problems*

Cardiovascular
Irregular pulse
Periods of rapid pulse
'Missing' heartbeats
Heart pounding
Skin cold and clammy
Skin blanching
Skin reddening
Hot and cold flashes
Throbbing

Respiratory
Unable to 'get enough air'
Sighing
Shortness of breath
Pressure or heavy feeling in chest
Chest pains
Breathlessness
Tightness in chest

Skeleto-muscular
Trembling
Shaking
Muscle tension
Muscle cramps
Muscle weakness
Grinding teeth
Muscle twitching
Excessive pressure when writing or
   similar task
Eye blinking
Strained facial muscles
Tension headaches
Wobbly, 'rubber legs'
Temporary loss of speech
Rapid/voluble speech
Stuttering

Alimentary and excretory
Dry mouth
Lump in throat
Difficulty swallowing
Retching
Nausea
Stomach rumbling or upset
'Butterflies in stomach'
'Knot' in stomach

Wind
Diarrhoea
Constipation
Retention of urine
Frequency or frequent urge to
   urinate

Sleep and relaxation
Delayed sleep onset
Waking in night
Waking early
Bad dreams, nightmares
Light sleep
Restlessness
Inability to relax
Pacing

Auditory, balance, visuo-spatial
Blurred vision
Narrowed vision
Unbalanced
Spinning
Veering to one side
Unsteady
Ringing in ears
Temporary hearing loss

Other anomalous bodily experiences
Tingling
Numbness
Bodily pains
Tiredness
Lightheadedness
Faintness

Anomalous mental experiences
Feeling distant from world
Feel self to be unreal, robotic
Loss of concentration
Easily distracted
Memory lapse for familiar things
Unable to dismiss unpleasant
   thoughts
Excessive worry about minor things
Difficulty thinking
Mind goes blank

counselling and his/her understanding of, and motivation for, the present form of counselling;

6 to obtain a more detailed account of the problems for which the client is seeking help (their history, current impact, future implications, frequency, duration and situational specificity).

A rigid structure for the interview is not implied by the above, because much valuable information comes out incidentally without disturbing the flow of conversation. The counsellor should take notes or make an audio-recording of the interview.

Self-report assessment of main problem areas

Checklists and questionnaires are a useful way of surveying a wide range of potential difficulties in advance of the first interview. The client can be asked to amplify on problems identified in this way. Some commonly used self-administered questionnaires are given in Appendix A. A checklist of fears and anxieties is given in Table 5.1. A list of mental and bodily signs that often accompany anxiety problems, grouped by bodily functions, is given in Table 5.2.

The main problems are elicited in the first 10-15 minutes of the initial interview, usually leading off from the contents of a referral letter. An *absence* of a desired behaviour is as much a problem as the presence of complaints and difficulties the client would prefer to be without. Exploration in depth is left until later in the interview.

Expanded account of main problems

Chronology

It is important to obtain an accurate chronology of events relating to the main problems as this might suggest their cause or, conversely, rule out some explanations. Clients may refer to a year or to their age to date an event, or may only be able to give a sequence while being hazy about timing. A sheet of paper with the columns drawn as in Table 5.3 is useful for recording this information.

The purpose here is to establish

a possible causal connection between events;
a repeated pattern or theme in the content of problems;
a fluctuation in problem frequency or severity and its associated events;
cyclical effects of a possibly physiological nature;
finally, to get a narrative sense of a client's life story.

Table 5.3 *A useful format for life history information*

Date	Age of client	Event and surrounding circumstances

The client's response to previous interventions may assist in evaluating motivation, preference for type of interventions, and which kind of intervention is most likely to be successful. If a definite onset for a problem can be established, then a detailed account of what happened at the time is valuable.

Current context and consequences of main problems
The purpose here is to place the problem(s) in the context of

- the situation in which they occur;
- what the client is thinking at the time;
- the immediate consequences; and
- the longer-term consequences.

Clients usually give a clearer account of the context when referring to concrete examples. Questions may be phrased as follows:

'Tell me about the last time you felt distressed in this way?' (or the first time, the worst time etc).
'Describe a typical day for me from the time you get up.'
'What's the first thing you notice with this problem?'
'What is going through your mind when this problem arises?'

Information about the context of the problem can be recorded as shown in Table 5.4.
As a way of eliciting the longer-term consequences, the following questions may be helpful.

'What will happen if the problem continues?'
'Does this problem prevent you doing anything?'
'How has your life changed since —?'

Table 5.4 *A useful format for functional analysis*

For each identified problem			
Situational antecedents	**Description of problem**	**Immediate consequences**	**Long-term consequences**
When, where, with whom	(1) Behaviour: Presence of .... Absence of .... (2) Sensations (3) Thoughts	Effect of response, change in situation, sensory or emotional consequences	Effect on others, withdrawal from activities, coping strategy, etc.

'What have you had to give up because of this problem?'
'What has this meant for (your partner, friends, family)?'
'What would you do if you were able to overcome this problem?'

The interview method of obtaining contextual information lacks the immediacy and spontaneity of direct observation. This can be achieved by one of the following methods

1 In the interview, use spontaneous or contrived incidents which highlight an anxiety theme, for example after obtaining the client's agreement, pretend to be someone with whom the client acts anxiously. Attempt to simulate a problematic encounter and ask the client how they are feeling and what they are thinking, or ask them to respond as they would normally.
2 Take the client to a situation which provokes distress in order to observe directly the client's behaviour and to obtain a report of their thinking processes.
3 Ask the client to imagine vividly the problem situation and describe what they are feeling, thinking or doing. Suggest alterations to the imaginary scenario to test out the importance of elements of the context. (This guided fantasy method is best conducted when the client is at least moderately relaxed and has his/her eyes closed.)

The thoughts that clients produce when describing anxiety-provoking imagery are often far more revealing of important aspects of the problem than information supplied cold and censored. In fact, clients are often surprised by the thoughts and images they produce. An example of an exploratory fantasy is given in the following pages. The analysis of contextual information obtained from this fantasy material and other sources is given in Table 5.5. It illustrates the phenomenon of chained thoughts leading to a catastrophic outcome described in chapter 4.

Extracts from an exploratory guided fantasy with a claustrophobic client (Cl = client, Co = Counsellor)

The client had panicked on a bus.

Transcript	*Commentary*
Cl: I normally catch this bus, which is never crowded. I normally get on downstairs but it was crowded because there was a bus strike. So I had to go upstairs.	
Co: How did you feel when you saw that?	Focus on sensations.
Cl: The bus really filled up. My mouth gets dry when I start thinking of things like this.	Imagery is already effective in producing fear.
Co: Your mouth is dry now, is it?	Focus on present to enhance reactions.
Cl: And all down the stairs there were lots of people and normally they can carry twenty standing but there must have been double that amount. They couldn't even shut the door.	Cl does not need prompting.
Co: Right, can you remember where you were sitting on the bus?	Focus on concrete detail to enhance image.
Cl: At the top of the stairs, the first seat behind.	
Co: And you were sitting next to someone?	More detail.
Cl: I was sitting next to a young woman. And we couldn't see out of the window with all the people breathing. No window open but it was cold. I opened the window –	

but the people behind shut it –
because I felt I couldn't breathe.
And I wiped the window so that I
could see out. When the bus started
to move off I felt a little bit more
relaxed. I thought at the next stop
people will start to get off but they
didn't. At the station there were
crowds of people coming out. Some
people were shouting they couldn't
get off, some couldn't get on.

Co: Just stop there for a moment. Now,   Focus on present.
can you tell me how you are feeling
right now? You said you had a dry
mouth, anything else?

Cl: A little bit apprehensive but not as
much as I was last night.

Co: Where do you feel apprehensive?   Elicit more detail.

Cl: In my chest, it feels tight.

Co: Your chest feels tight, OK. And you   Investigate.
said on the bus you couldn't
breathe very well?

Cl: Yes. I thought I must open the
window.

Co: When you said you couldn't   Press further.
breathe, what do you mean exactly?
What happened last night?

Cl: I was shut in.

Co: You felt shut in?   Reflect and wait.

Cl: Yes.

Co: What happened to your breathing,   Press still further.
though?

Cl: I felt I was suffocating.

Co: Suffocating? You couldn't get
enough . . .?

Cl: Enough air. That's why I wiped the
window with a tissue. Not that that
would do much good. Maybe look
out of the window and realize . . .
there was a window there.

Co: Did you feel that your breathing   Trying to elicit
had stopped?   thoughts.

Cl: Well, it feels like someone has got their hands around your throat and choking you. Not that I've had anybody's hands around my throat. It's imagination, sort of thing.

Co pursued this line of questioning a little longer without success. (Fear of suffocation later turned out to be of etiological significance.)

[*A few moments later*]

Cl: Well, I get these palpitations, that my heart's beating faster and then my hands get clammy. I want to rush off. I want to get up and rush down the stairs and get out.

This is the classic escape response.

Co: Did you feel that last night, that you wanted to rush downstairs?

Cl: I did, but it went off because I spoke to the woman next to me to try to take my mind off the situation.

Cl uses distraction.

Co: I want you to imagine that situation again as vividly as you can. You're on top of the bus, upstairs, people standing in the stairway.

Co tries to strengthen the image and emotion to bring out her thoughts.

Cl: Yes, and all along the side of me.

Co: So you're surrounded by people. Now I want you to imagine those feelings. You can't get enough air, your throat feels dry, your heart's beating faster, your hands are sweating. Try to feel that, thinking 'I can't get out of here'; 'I can't even see out of the window'; 'I can't even open the window'; 'I feel like rushing out.'

Emphasize present tense.

Cl: Yes.

Co: Try to imagine those feelings. Try to experience them all over again. Your chest is feeling tight now. Your heart is beating faster. You're thinking to yourself 'How can I get out of here'. You're stuck there, stuck on the seat. If you wanted to get out, you couldn't do it very easily. You'd have to push past all those people. Imagine this and describe what you experience.

Cl: It's not very pleasant. I've not got the palpitations like I had with the real thing. But the dryness of the mouth is there. But I haven't got the runaway feeling.

Co: Fine. When you were on the bus you tried to distract yourself by talking to the person next to you. Describe the thoughts you were distracting yourself from.

Ask for thoughts now that she is really involved.

Cl: Well, I'm thinking to myself: This is ridiculous I've got this terrible feeling of being shut in. I've got to fight this and I'll talk to this woman because I won't be able to get off anyway.

Co: Now this is what you did in order to overcome your fear and fight it. That's fine. But you did that to take your mind off your sensations. Is that right?

Checking validity of the facts. Pressing further.

Cl: Yes, I didn't want to make myself look a fool.

A thought elicited!

Co: Right.

Cl: Because I have been in a situation where I've been shut in, in a flat. And that went through my mind. My friend forgot I have claustrophobia, so she went outside, shut me in, she was about eight floors up and I couldn't open the door. And *she* couldn't open the door. I sat behind the door crouched down like a little child calling to get help. And I didn't want that same situation again. That's what was going through my mind.

Cl recalls what she actually thought on the theme of being a fool.

Co: Right, that went through your mind last night?

Cl: Yes. And that happened eight or nine years ago.

Co: So you were crouched down there. What were you thinking about then, behind the door?

Shift to the past traumatic memory and pursue its meaning.

Cl: Just praying that someone would hurry up and come to let me out. And they broke the door down.

Co: You said you didn't want to feel a fool – did you feel a fool then?

Echo earlier thought.

Cl: Yes, but nobody laughed at me when they opened the door.

Co: But you felt a fool yourself?

Cl: Yes I did.

Co: And your friend didn't think so?

Cl: She was very upset when she forgot I have claustrophobia.

Cl: I'd completely forgotten about that till last night.

Inaccessible memory returning during intense emotion.

Self-observation

Some therapeutic interventions are conducted within a procedure of fantasy creation, and these will be illustrated in chapter 6. Another method of assessment is *self-monitoring*. Clients are given the task of observing their own thoughts, feelings and actions between sessions, and recording this information in a diary, which takes the form of the first three columns in Table 5.5. Further guidance on the use of diaries can be found in chapter 7. It is rare for a client to produce a perfect diary record from the beginning. Praise should be given for whatever is produced, followed by suggestions for improving the quality of the information. As it becomes apparent that a diary is a valuable tool, it assumes greater importance to the client.

Self-monitoring merges into an intervention in its own right (see chapter 7) and in most forms of intervention it has a subsidiary role in teaching clients to become more aware of a problem and its context, and also in monitoring the transfer of learning from an office-based intervention to day-to-day life. Information collected in a diary is analysed and discussed at the beginning of the session.

Table 5.5 *Functional analysis of contextual material from guided fantasy*

Situational antecedents	Description of problem	Short-term consequences	Long-term consequences
Sitting on bus Exit restricted by people in aisles	1 Behaviour – urge to get off bus 2 Sensations/ feelings – dry mouth, chest tight, palpitations, suffocation 3 Thoughts – I will look a fool by acting like a child and screaming out for help	Talked to distract self Eventually escaped to safety	Constant apprehension about entering enclosed places Avoidance of some forms of public transport Loss of self-esteem Strain on marriage

The client is normally asked to give an expanded account. Attention may be drawn to elements in the context that may not have seemed significant at the time. The quality of diary recording improves as the client is better able to discriminate events of importance.

Episodes recorded in the diary can be viewed as natural experiments in which the outcome supports one or other formulation of the problem. For example, a couple on holiday found that they related much better to each other and enjoyed making love far more than they had done for many months. On returning home, the woman tensed up before lovemaking and was disgusted and distressed when her partner insisted on making love to her when she did not want to herself. An analysis of the contrasting episodes revealed that lovemaking on holiday was 'spontaneous' and occurred during the daytime. At home, lovemaking usually occurred in the evening and was 'expected' by her partner. She had developed what she described as a 'phobia' for the evening.

The woman had always felt emotionally manipulated and controlled by her mother, and a request of whatever nature in which she felt her freedom of choice restricted was extremely aversive to her. A discussion of these diary episodes led her to formulate her 'sexual anxiety problems' in a new way. That is, she revealed that making love was not intrinsically unpleasurable for her (that she did not have a 'hang-up' about sex), but that the manner in which her partner approached her was crucial to her enjoyment. As noted above, she linked her tension to any situation in which she felt undue 'emotional pressure' was being exerted on her to comply with a request.

The new formulation increased her motivation to discuss the difficulty in her sexual relationship with her partner, something which she had formerly resisted because her 'problem' had seemed intractable. It is clear from this example how self-monitoring developed into a method of intervention based on homework tasks.

Diagrammatic depiction of a client's problems

Drawing a diagram to show how events in a client's life relate to each other can be useful to the counsellor as a way of making explicit preliminary formulations. A diagram of this kind can be shared with the client, not only to find out whether it is an accurate representation of the client's problems, but also to foster a joint understanding and make apparent the reasons for intervening in a certain way.

The elements in the diagram are in themselves summaries of observations or shorthand expressions, and they may include general dispositions like 'under-assertiveness'. The diagram is inevitably speculative and causal connections cannot in most cases be established. It is assumed simply that the elements affect each other or lead to one another. The influence of one element on another is assumed to be that of causing it to get worse either by *increasing* its magnitude/frequency, or by *suppressing* its occurrence or frequency. The helpful effects of positive elements can also be represented. Past events are influential because they may determine expectations in current situations. Similarly, anticipation of future events influences current behaviour. The diagram therefore represents events in a mental 'space-time', that does, nevertheless, concern real events that can be changed, or real events that have the power to change mental representations.

All of this is best illustrated by way of a case example. A verbal description will be given first, before attempting a diagrammatic depiction of the problem (see Figure 5.1). Mrs J. is a recently married computer programmer in her mid-twenties. Her husband is an executive who works long hours and often travels abroad. Mrs J.'s firm has asked her to complete a project within an over-ambitious deadline. She takes on the work but feels stressed. Her mental concentration suffers and she experiences a 'panic attack' at work. Her pulse races, her hands shake and she is unable to focus on the keyboard. She experiences an irresistible urge to rush out of the office, which she does. She returns later but still finds it difficult to concentrate. A week later 'panic' recurs and she returns home on the excuse of illness.

At home she becomes increasingly agitated, unable to decide whether to return to work, experiencing daily episodes of panic. Her general practitioner, recognizing her extreme agitation, and chronic indecision, takes the unusual step of having her admitted for a short stay in an acute ward of a psychiatric unit. It transpires that this doctor had treated Mrs J's father for depression, but he had committed suicide while in his care. The doctor is understandably cautious, and does not wish to take any chances with his patient. The doctor colludes with the client's false account of herself as having 'a viral illness' so that neither her employer nor relatives knows the real reason for her admission to hospital.

Mrs J. spends a considerable amount of time with her mother, who is emotionally supportive but gets drawn into her daughter's inability to make a decision about her job – whether to return or resign. Moreover, her mother is as worried about her daughter as the daughter is herself about her own condition. Her mother has an intense fear that her daughter is becoming mentally ill like her husband. Mrs J.'s own husband is unable to be very supportive of his wife because of his long working hours. He is rather matter of fact and suggests that she give up her work. Mrs J. is upset that he does not respond in a more emotionally reassuring manner.

At first interview Mrs J. describes specific forms of somatic distress as well as providing evidence for being chronically highly aroused. She feels 'uptight' most of the time, bites her nails badly, is unable to concentrate, relax or get off to sleep quickly. She shows extreme vacillation in choice situations, especially where her job is concerned. Somatic distress includes hot sweats, cramp-like chest pains, and 'butterflies in the stomach'. She reports her self-confidence as 'very low', feels 'lazy' because she is not working, and also guilty about the consequences of her problem on her mother and husband.

When asked how she would like to see herself, she replies 'well organized, competent, achieving, and not lazy'. Academic achievement has always been important in her family and although she had finally obtained a university degree, this had been a struggle. She had extra private tuition as a child and had always experienced great stress under the pressure of examinations. Apart from this, she had never been particularly anxious in other situations and had never sought or received help of a psychological kind. She does not regard herself as 'academically bright' and wishes she had a first-rate brain. High standards are important to her, and she feels she is letting herself and others down if she sacrifices them. Precision and orderliness are highly valued.

Mrs J. valued her competence, and others' opinion of it, so highly that she found it very difficult to turn down requests to undertake extra work. In this respect, but not in others, she was under-assertive. She acknowledged that she was good at her work, regarded by others as competent, and that her supervisor's abilities were generally inferior to her own. However, this knowledge did not permit her to ease up on the standards she demanded of herself.

Mrs J. was clearly unable to continue working while remaining as distressed as she had recently become. An exploration of the meaning to her of resigning from her job helped to explain why she was so much in conflict over giving it up or retaining it. In effect, a cognitive analysis was performed as described in chapter 4. To resign would imply to her that she was all the things she disvalued – being poorly organized, incompetent, unachieving and lazy. To see things in this way is an example of irrational thinking – that this decision would reflect on her whole personality for all time (over-generalization) rather than represent a temporary setback following which she would be able to regain her former status in a new job. Instead, the consequences of resigning were associated by her with two catastrophic scenarios: (1) that she would be seen as failing as a professional person in the eyes of her husband and his family, and that this might in turn lead to a breakdown of the marriage (she already felt critically scrutinized by her husband's parents and was concerned about proving her worth); (2) that if she resigned from her job this meant that she was 'stupid' and also unable to cope with life, like her father. There was a fear that she would break down and become mentally ill. This fear was reinforced by the worries expressed by her mother and general practitioner.

This general outline of Mrs J.'s problem can be represented graphically as shown in Figure 5.1, which demonstrates:

- the complexity of anxiety problems and the interrelation of past, present and future events, real or imagined;
- the role of intimate associates of the client either in reinforcing anxieties or in failing to provide a source of safety/security;
- that an intervention may entail making difficult existential decisions (e.g. to resign or not from well-paid employment);

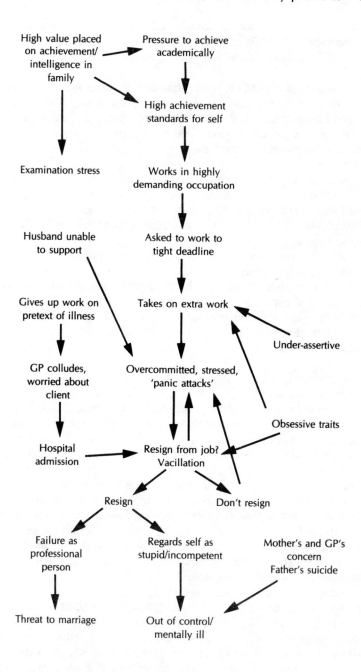

Figure 5.1 *Complex anxiety problem*

– that a problem can be influenced at multiple points in this complex web of interconnected behaviours, thoughts, physiological reactions, decisions, values and relationships.

I will not at this point state what interventions were attempted or even mention the outcome. I will simply point out some possible interventions to illustrate how the interrelated elements can be influenced in different ways. The suggestions are not necessarily recommended for this woman.

– Influence client's achievement standards.
– Teach client control of panic attacks.
– Modify irrational thinking and catastrophization.
– Marriage counselling: e.g. encourage husband to be more supportive.
– Influence attitudes of mother and GP towards client.
– Teach assertiveness.
– Encourage client to give up job and make a new start in a less stressful occupation.
– Teach relaxation and management of stress.
– Suggest the client obtains tranquillizing medication and goes back to work.

Vicious cycles and anxiety complaints
Figure 5.1 illustrates how vicious cycles of events can make a bad situation worse still. As Mrs J. became more distressed as the result of her conflict over resigning or staying in her job, she experienced even greater bodily arousal and mental inefficiency. This indicated that she really was becoming 'mentally ill', unable to work, and hence, incompetent and stupid. She saw her marriage breaking down and herself in a low-status job. She may not have been aware of these thoughts as she began to feel panicky, but cognitive analysis suggested that these beliefs were operating. It is assumed that the thoughts occurred briefly and automatically, or perhaps flashed through the mind as an image. This is a short-term vicious cycle which takes the general form depicted in Figure 5.2. Examples are given in Figure 5.3.

Longer-term vicious cycles arise out of the environmental consequences of an anxiety problem. Mrs J. found it difficult to entertain the prospect of giving up work and losing the self-esteem derived from her professional status. Her husband did not know how to help and the relationship became strained. The mother and general practitioner tended to reinforce the client's view of herself. It is not too difficult to imagine how a deteriorating situation developed.

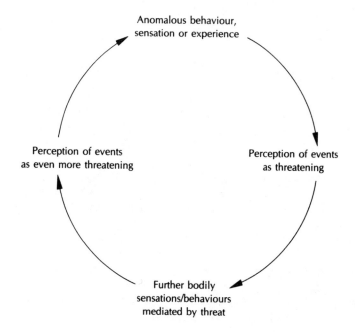

Figure 5.2   *Short-term vicious cycle in anxiety problems*

Setting targets and choosing the order of interventions

The assessment process leads to the point at which:

– decisions are made about the targets of counselling;
– the problem is formulated (provisionally);
– preferred modes of intervention are selected;
– the order in which interventions are carried out is decided.

The basis for making these decisions will be explained and illustrated in later chapters.

Suggestions for further reading

For further guidance on the assessment interview see Kirk (1989) and Trower et al. (1988). Barker (1985) is a down-to-earth guide to behavioural assessment. A variety of practical cognitive assessment techniques are described in Beck et al. (1985).

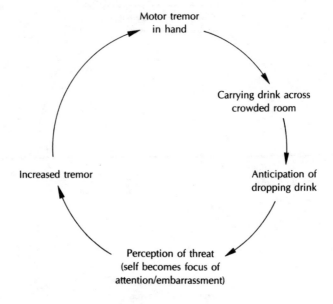

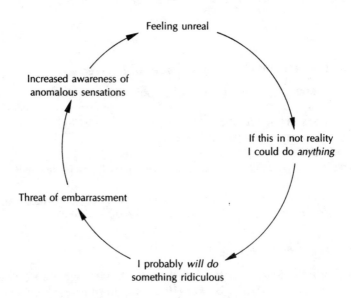

Figure 5.3   *Examples of short-term vicious cycles*

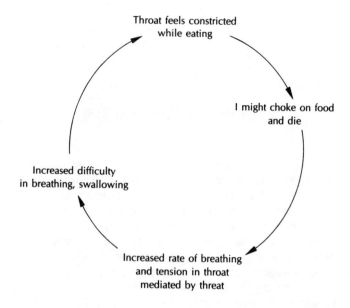

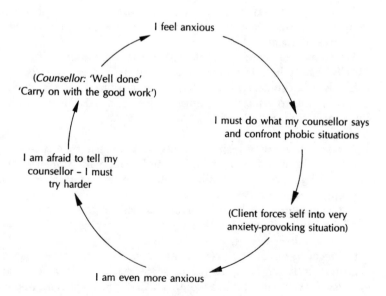

Figure 5.3   *Examples of short-term vicious cycles* (cont.)

6

Principles of Confrontation

Interventions can be divided into those that are designed to change *responses* to specific cues and those that aim to change *responsivity* to a wider range of situations. In the latter category fall relaxation classes, teaching problem-solving skills, and assertiveness training.

I am at present concerned with the first category of intervention. An essential component of the modification of fear and anxiety is that some means of *confronting* the situation is required to allow relearning to occur. Relearning may emphasize the acquisition of new ways of responding or, alternatively, unlearning old ways. Fear responses may be triggered by *internal* (self-produced) cues such as sensations arising from over-breathing, or by *external* cues. An important class of self-produced cues is that associated with anxiety itself. It may be necessary to *provoke* anxiety deliberately in order for the client to confront these cues and unlearn their responses to them.

We know that confrontation with anxiety-provoking situations usually results in a lessening of the distress a client reports, but there is still considerable debate about what happens during confrontation to effect the change. Some proposals for explaining the process are as follows:

1 *Extinction*. Anxiety responses may be mediated by an expectation that something harmful or unpleasant will happen if the provoking situation is confronted. The expectation may be simply that 'anxiety' will escalate to an intolerable level, and this constitutes the harm. For clients who expect an escalation of this kind, noticing the first signs of 'anxiety' is the provoking situation that gives rise to the expectation. Extinction is the technical term for the process that weakens a response when a reinforcer is removed. In the present case, the reinforcer is an aversive event (some harm or other). Confrontation is an opportunity to learn that this harm does not arise or is not as bad as imagined.

2 *Habituation*. This process refers to weakening a reflexive or

innate response by repeated exposure to the same stimulus. For example, a startle reflex to a sudden loud sound habituates if the sound is repeated. In the therapeutic sense, habituation refers to a similar process of the weakening of responses (including startle, orienting and fear reflexes) through repeated familiarity with the same situation.

3 *Acquisition of coping skills.* Confrontation allows a person to learn how to respond adaptively. for example dealing effectively with a hostile remark. The potential threat is removed through the acquisition of a coping response. One category of coping skills involves learning how to quell anxiety responses themselves. For example, adopting a relaxed posture and breathing more slowly is a skill that can be learned and applied deliberately.

4 *Cognitive change.* As will be illustrated later, a person learns to reconstrue the provoking situation so that it appears less threatening. The client may discover hidden resources for dealing with a threat, the presumed cause of a threat may be reattributed to an innocuous event, the likelihood or severity of a threat may be reappraised, and so forth. Cognitive change can occur through verbal interchange with a client or through a 'behavioural experiment' in which a client's familiar assumptions about the world may be contradicted by the consequences of acting in new ways.

5 *Reciprocal inhibition.* Certain behaviours tend to inhibit anxiety responses. These include acting angrily, consuming food, and deliberately relaxing. Confrontation may be arranged to evoke an anxiety and inhibitory response together so that the former is weakened.

What follows is a set of guidelines for designing a programme of confrontation that optimizes the beneficial operation of these hypothetical processes. The design and implementation of a programme can be broken down into several steps:

- assessing the stimulus dimensions;
- choosing the starting point;
- selecting a medium of confrontation;
- orienting the client for effective confrontation;
- planning a therapy session;
- spacing of sessions;
- terminating the programme.

Assessing the stimulus dimensions

In most cases we have a good idea of what thoughts, images, objects or situations elicit the problem. It may not be obvious *why* a stimulus elicits distress but the fact that it does so is indicated by subjective discomfort, behavioural inhibition, tendency to escape and other bodily reactions. The majority of anxiety problems can be related to a limited number of themes or stimulus dimensions. The first task is to identify these themes and, for each one, to make up a list of situations, real or imaginary, that relate to it. With imaginal confrontation techniques (see p. 82) there need be no constraint on thematic content. However, if confrontation is going to take place in actual situations, then it is preferable to list situations that can be realized through direct contact, simulation, or role-play.

After grouping into themes, the situations in each one are rated by the client for the degree of distress they elicit, and the items are rank ordered on this basis. This list is known as an *anxiety hierarchy*. A 0–10 scale is convenient for rating, where 0 = 'not at all distressing' and 10 = 'as distressed/anxious/panicky as I have ever been'. (Definition of the anchoring points may depend on the way the problem is expressed.) Clients may not be able to estimate how distressed they will become in a situation. This is not surprising for situations that have been completely avoided in the past. Clients may find it easier to judge their reactions if they close their eyes and develop a fantasy of entering the situation. Alternatively, a client may be induced to approach the feared situation and to report on their distress as they get closer to it. This is referred to as a *behavioural test*. In any event, the rank ordering of hierarchy items should be regarded as provisional.

It is useful to rate each item for degree of avoidance (e.g. 'would not avoid', 'slightly avoid', 'generally avoid', 'always avoid'). The anxiety and avoidance ratings of hierarchy items can be used to evaluate progress. Re-rating of the original items can be useful to demonstrate to a client that progress has been made.

Hierarchy items should be described concretely to remove any ambiguity about the meaning of the situation. For example, 'driving on the motorway between X town and Y town' is preferable to 'driving on motorways'. This will enhance the validity of the item as a measure of progress. An example of a hierarchy is given in Table 6.1.

The critical elicitors of anxiety responses are not always identified early on in assessment and may only come to light as confrontation is implemented. Close observation of a client's non-

Table 6.1 *Example of a fear/anxiety hierarchy relating to moths*

Items in hierarchy (ranked)	Fear/anxiety rating (0–10)
Dead fly	2
Small dead moth	4
Butterflies on the wing in field	5
Large dead moth	6
Butterfly in same room as client	7
Small live moth in glass jar	7
Butterfly alighting on client's hair	8
Large live moth in glass jar	8
Large moth flying in room	10
Large moth alighting on client's hair	10

verbal behaviour during confrontation may indicate the relevance of particular cues. Clients should be encouraged to provide as much information as possible about thoughts or stimulus elements that seem significant to them.

The initial ranking should be regarded as provisional. Items can be re-rated at intervals, preferably in the presence of the actual item. Ratings may be used to monitor progress and to guide the planning of a confrontation session. In the latter case, it is probable that new items will have to be devised to grade confrontation more smoothly, for example creating movement in dead moths by tossing from hand to hand and inducing contact with small moths in stages.

Choosing the starting point

In choosing a starting point, there are two critical questions: which hierarchy, and where in the hierarchy to begin? Some criteria for choosing broader objectives and the order of intervention have been described in chapter 5. Of chief importance are: the extent to which the anxiety theme interferes in a client's life and is important to the client; and the extent to which success can be obtained relatively quickly, thereby motivating the client to greater effort.

The point in the hierarchy at which confrontation begins depends partly on the method. However, it is worth noting some theoretical considerations here. Reducing anxiety associated with one hierarchy is unlikely to impact on others, and so an intervention for each anxiety theme will probably be required. However, *within* a hierarchy, reducing anxiety to one item generalizes to other items. If, for example, a middle-ranking item is confronted first, the client will respond less anxiously to items lower in the hierarchy even though they have never been dealt with directly. At some point the highest items should be confronted, otherwise upon encountering the situation in future (or re-experiencing it in fantasy), the client's anxieties are likely to become resensitized.

When certain traumatic memories, (such as a car crash) are still very upsetting, it may be necessary to incorporate elements of the memory in the confrontation technique. However, confrontation of situations associated with the memory (e.g. visiting a hospital or cemetery, driving a car at speed on a motorway) may be sufficient to reduce its power to evoke distress.

In principle there is no major theoretical objection to beginning high up in the hierarchy ranking, but in practice certain conditions should be fulfilled, as follows:

A client should feel confident that he/she can tackle the item. Unforced willingness to proceed must be ensured. Some gentle persuasion is permissible, but the client should have the final say. Clients are usually able to state with conviction what they think they can achieve but the counsellor should be aware of over-confidence. Once clients understand the general approach, they may spontaneously suggest the next step. Alternatively, a counsellor might ask 'What are you ready for next?'

The nature of the confrontation should be clearly spelled out for the client. The unexpected introduction of new fearful elements is counterproductive and may lead to a setback. Clients should be told: 'Some people find this distressing; you may feel like leaving the session – is that all right with you?' Remind the client at the beginning: 'We can stop this at any moment if you feel it is too distressing, so don't hold back from letting me know.' 'We can take this as slowly as you like – it's important that you feel confident at each step.' The counsellor should always adhere to the planned agenda for the session.

When a counsellor is unsure how a client will react, confrontation should begin low down on the hierarchy. For example, a client phobic of spiders might begin with a line drawing of a spider. Progression up the hierarchy can proceed more rapidly if an item is not at all or only very mildly distressing.

If the counsellor begins with a highly anxiety-provoking item, it is essential that sufficient time is allocated to the session for the client to learn to tolerate the item with less anxiety.

Sometimes the introduction of a highly distressing situation cannot be avoided. For example, it may be impossible to confront a traumatic memory in a graded manner. As noted earlier, an important component of the anxiety-provoking situation may be the experience of being highly aroused subjectively and physiologically. Gradual methods that do not allow a client to confront a 'major panic' would be ineffective because they do not expose the client to critical internal cues. Nevertheless, interventions are always carefully structured and planned to ensure that they are manageable for the client.

Selecting a medium of confrontation

A client can be asked to *imagine* an anxiety-provoking situation or *actually confront* it in real, simulated or audio/visually recorded forms. A confrontation procedure can be managed and led by the counsellor or be self-managed by the client. Typically, both methods are employed.

Pragmatic considerations influence the selection of a confrontational technique as follows:

1 If the client possesses little or no imagery ability, fantasy material is unlikely to act as an effective stimulus.
2 Where the critical elicitors cannot be reproduced or simulated in real life, fantasy become indispensable (e.g. certain social, sexual, death or illness situations). Nevertheless, it is usually possible to devise a self-managed programme which incorporates the critical situations in real life.
3 When the client is extremely fearful and cannot entertain the thought of real-life confrontation, a gradual approach with imaginal/symbolic material can be adopted. Further guidelines are offered at the end of this chapter where particular methods are described.

Orienting the client for effective confrontation

The client should receive an explanation of the approach, as mentioned earlier, along with suitable reading matter where it seems appropriate. Clients vary a great deal in how they show distress and how they feel about another person witnessing them in such a state. The same counsellor, apparently adopting the same manner, can be perceived by one client as a detached, distant expert and by another as warm and empathic. These individual differences in the quality of the relationship influence the approach a counsellor takes with a particular client. There are some general guidelines for preparing all clients:

1   Do not introduce a distressing technique until rapport and trust have been established and the client understands the rationale.

2   Be clear about the objectives for a session but build in flexibility. For example, be prepared to change the agenda if a temporary crisis has developed or the client's mood is unusually low.

3   Attempt to discriminate between genuinely fearful reluctance and procrastination or lack of effort.

4   Let the client know that you expect him/her to become distressed.

5   Act in a confident and relaxed manner so that the client feels you are prepared for any eventuality. The client is trained in relaxation for some confrontational techniques (see p. 82) but it is by no means essential or always helpful to prepare a client by beginning a session with a relaxation exercise.

6   During the session, the eliciting situation or fantasy should hold the client's attention: turning away or otherwise negating the impact of the situation is discouraged. One way to maintain attention is to ask the client to describe the most notable features of the situation and to itemize their own reactions. The appropriate mental set could be described as one of fully accepting what is happening with an attitude of detached curiosity. Clients who deny the threatening aspects of the situation, perceive it as 'unreal', keep their reactions under strict control or divert their attention elsewhere are less likely to experience a diminution of their anxiety. This may happen if the client is not ready for the items selected; the counsellor should revert to an item lower in the hierarchy. Alternatively, the counsellor draws the client's attention to the defensive strategy, prompts a different response, explains the rationale again, and so on.

7   Help the client reframe the experience. The purpose of encouraging detached curiosity is to help the client reinterpret his/her experiences in the framework of normal psychological and physiological processes. Understanding what makes up the rather vaguely defined state of 'anxiety' and knowing what features of a situation arouse it increases a client's sense of the predictability and control of these phenomena. The client will soon discover and acquire faith in the fact that the reactions subside over a relatively short period of time. The client is encouraged to reattribute the cause of their distressing experiences to short-lived, natural processes produced by specific situations and to avoid making the inference that their response to anxiety reflects on them in a

global, permanent and negative way. For example, some clients believe that behaving anxiously implies weaknesses, neurosis or stupidity. To assist in the process of reattribution, a counsellor can remind the client that:

> 'The rapid pulse you are experiencing is due to effects of the hormone adrenalin.'
> 'From what I can see, you are experiencing the peak of your panic but if you wait, it will fade and pass.'
> 'I am sure that your anxiety is extremely unpleasant but it will not physically harm you.'
> 'I expect you are feeling more fearful now because your escape routes are blocked and you feel trapped.'

The client is invited to ask questions about the nature and changing quality of their experiences. In turn, the counsellor asks the client to explain the same phenomena. In this way, knowledge of the determinants of anxiety is imparted, and clients begin to respond to their own thoughts and feelings with more helpful self-observations.

Planning a therapy session

As a general rule, the more intense the response to the hierarchy item, the longer it will take for the client to master the situation and achieve a satisfactorily calm state. Some confrontation techniques use short exposures measured in seconds or minutes, while in others the duration of exposure is from forty minutes to several hours. Short-duration confrontation of highly anxiety-provoking situations, especially if followed by immediate escape, is likely to sensitize the client and strengthen his/her appraisal of it as threatening and unpleasant. In order to achieve a *desensitizing* effect it is important to maintain a long duration of exposure to the same situation, allowing time for the client to manage their reactions to the threat. Guidelines for determining the duration of confrontation are given below. As a general rule, a counsellor should avoid introducing items (for example, at the end of session) when there is insufficient time to process them.

Within any given episode of confrontation (e.g. single-hierarchy items) there are likely to be elements that can be manipulated to intensify or ameliorate its impact. This is easily achieved with imaginal material where the possibilities for modifying a scene are almost infinite. In a real-life confrontation with an animal such as a dog, the animal can be induced to be more or less lively, to be positioned with its head to the client or vice versa and so forth. It is important to anticipate these various possibilities when planning the session. In some methods of confrontation, progression up the hierarchy proceeds without rigid advanced planning; judgement is exercised moment to moment in the light of the client's responses. The essence of these judgements is that confrontation is graded, repeated and prolonged until the client achieves calmness and a sense of mastery.

The following guidelines are offered to help the counsellor determine the speed of progression up the hierarchy and duration of confrontation:

1   The client's distress has reduced to a low and manageable level. Level of distress can be estimated from behavioural signs, the client's self-report, and by asking at intervals for 0–10 ratings of distress. Although there are no hard and fast rules, the duration should be prolonged until the client rates no more than 3 to 4 out of 10. (In the method of imagined desensitization, minimal or zero levels must be reached before progressing to the next item.)

There is some disagreement on whether allowing a client to escape from the situation when distress mounts undoes any gain that has been made. Whether this is true probably depends on the spirit in which confrontation is approached and how clients appraise their performance. Clients who hold the view that courage, patience and persistence will allow them to attain their goal (and believe they are capable of attaining it) may perceive fearful encounters from which they have 'escaped fearfully' as a 'success'. This is true especially of situations never before entered (e.g. entering a large shop for the first time) which are expected to be distressing. On the contrary, unexpected anxiety in a situation previously mastered is more likely to damage confidence and lead to a revision of estimates of threat and increased caution. 'Setbacks' of this kind are more likely to happen in self-managed interventions. They should not happen in a planned session if it has been well prepared and potential problems have been anticipated. If a client does retreat hastily in a planned session, the counsellor should encourage a gradual return to the feared situation. The close monitoring of a client's distress by the method of repeated self-rating decreases the likelihood of an unexpected increase in anxiety.

2   All varying stimulus elements within an item should be exploited and the item should be repeated so that the reduction in distress is fully consolidated before moving on to the next items. For example, in a self-managed programme of travel by train, the client should have encountered and tolerated short train stops in a tunnel.

3   A spontaneous return of fear or anxiety should be expected to occur over the interval between sessions. For this reason, at the beginning of a session, confrontation should commence at a hierarchy level *lower* than the final level reached in the previous session.

4   A related point to bear in mind is that a client's tolerance for distress, and the background level of that distress, fluctuates from day to day. Some clients show very marked fluctuations. There may, or may not, be any discernible pattern in this. A counsellor should be sensitive to a client's fragility or resilience on a particular day.

5   Clients may benefit from short respites throughout a session. There should be time to reflect on the experience, regain composure, or simply take a rest.

Spacing of sessions

The length of the interval between sessions depends, in part, on the nature of the problem. In self-managed programmes the pace is determined largely by the client. When the stimulus cues are circumscribed and do not depend on frequently occurring events in the client's life, sessions can be more closely spaced. Long intervals are a disadvantage because the client spends more time awaiting the next session, in some cases with anxious anticipation. Two or three sessions a week can be planned, depending on the availability of counsellor and client. In largely self-managed programmes the role of the counsellor is different, and the interval between sessions is more likely to be 1–4 weeks, or even longer as time goes on. The client confronts situations regularly on the basis of agreed homework tasks. Spacing of sessions is determined by the frequency with which significant eliciting situations are encountered or can be engineered.

Terminating the programme

Clients usually have a good idea of the end-point they want to reach. It normally coincides with the ending of restrictions on their day-to-day life. Some examples are being able to take a holiday flight, being able to shop in preferred stores, or being able to open the windows of a house on summer nights when moths are flying.

A client may be considered to have progressed satisfactorily when they are unlikely to encounter a situation which could precipitate an unpleasant degree of distress, bearing in mind that hazardous and threatening situations cannot be ruled out altogether.

It is desirable for clients to *overlearn* their mastery of anxiety-provoking situations (for example to tolerate extremely busy High Street shops they rarely visit normally), even though encountering such a situation is unlikely. This rule should be applied with caution to situations that are naturally hazardous, such as driving at speed on a motorway.

It is sensible to work towards feasible, attainable and personally gratifying targets. Achieving one target encourages the client to attempt another, so that progress follows a stepwise function. Targets are increasingly initiated and met by the client working autonomously. It is usual to arrange follow-up contacts to provide advice, as required, or help to deal with setbacks.

Additional observations on mastery of anxiety

Clients' structuring of the experiences

Inducing a client to confront anxiety-provoking situations is necessary, but not always sufficient to produce a lessening of distress. What the client makes of the experience and how the encounter can be arranged to increase a client's sense of mastery are important. The aim is to foster confidence in a general ability to cope despite variation in circumstances. Clients who attribute their successful confrontation to the fact that they had their eyes closed, to the presence of the therapist close at hand, to the use of a tranquillizing drug or to the fact that confrontation occurred on a 'good day' will have fewer grounds for acquiring a stable belief in their ability to master anxiety in the situation. This is not to say, of course, that a strong sense of confidence can be achieved without intermediate stages of semi-mastery in which some reliance is placed on additional help. Any crutch is permissible as long as it is a means to an end and can be discarded later. A counsellor can assist the client to develop mastery by:

- showing how difficult situations can be tackled by breaking them down into intermediate steps;
- suggesting how safety signals can be employed and then gradually faded out;
- helping the client plan for all untoward eventualities, in terms of either direct action or tactical retreat (e.g. 'escape routes');
- analysing any defensive manoeuvre the client may be using to partially or totally avoid situations and to suggest how the client can relinquish it;
- modelling a step in the programme, e.g. handling a spider while the client observes.

Modifying defensive behaviours

The client's experience of fear, and tendency to escape from anxiety-provoking situations should decline as provoking situations are confronted. In some cases, however, the defensive response creates a vicious spiral of anxiety and means have to be found to break into this feedback process. The modification of rapid eating in the client described in chapter 4 illustrates this point. The following set of guidelines indicates how this might be achieved.

1 Reconstruing the threat   The aim here is not to divert attention from the situation *per se* but to reconstrue it in a non-threatening light, or to pay attention to features of it that are positively interesting. For a spider-phobic person, this might mean viewing spiders as would a naturalist. For someone fearful of public places, the person could be encouraged to pay attention to what is happening in a street, to trees or flowers or to objects in shop windows.

2 Deliberate relaxation   A client can facilitate calmness by deliberately modifying postural and other bodily responses. The counsellor may have to point out when and how this can be done, but as time goes on, clients normally become aware of their tendency to tense up and initiate remedial action. The client is advised to:

– adopt a relaxed posture generally;
– unclench fingers;
– relax hunched-up shoulders;
– slow down the rate of breathing.

Some clients benefit from being taught how to relax deeply. They can also be taught to apply a rapid relaxation manoeuvre when tensed up, or fearful (see chapter 8). The use of relaxation to counter particular defensive responses can be practised at first in the counsellor's office and then in provoking situations.

3 Prevention of the defensive response   An anxious client may produce involuntarily a response that has threatening consequences. For example, to experience a speech block while talking could lead to a concern about how one appears to others. A failure to become sexually aroused could lead to fears that a partner will react negatively and break off the relationship. To be unable to swallow could lead to a fear of choking. In each case, anticipation of the threatening consequence may result in an intensification of the original involuntary defensive response. It is impossible to list all the possible ways in which this feedback process can operate. The process may take place in a matter of seconds or minutes but the negative implications are perceived as disproportionately great. Two principles can be applied to circumvent this process:

1 Prevent or suppress the defensive response that has these negative consequences. The solution may be as simple as instructing a client to *pause* until ready to respond appropriately.
2 Actively assist the client in developing behaviour appropriate to the situation, thereby obviating the primary source of threat, e.g. teach assertive responses, public speaking skills, behaviour that facilitates sexual arousal.

Established techniques

Systematic desensitization

This technique was invented in the 1950s by Joseph Wolpe, one of the founders of the behaviour therapy school. It is most commonly associated with *imaginal* exposure of hierarchy items, and although this method has largely been supplanted by more rapidly effective real-life techniques, it still has valuable applications.

It is a very gradual approach and so the hierarchies typically have a large number of evenly spaced items. The client is first taught relaxation. An assumption underlying the original method was that relaxation reciprocally inhibits any anxious response to the imagined situation. Whether or not relaxation performs this function, or facilitates the procedure in other ways, is not entirely clear. However, in a relaxed state clients are better able to create vivid images and are more likely to discriminate the bodily effects of an image when their baseline level of physiological arousal is low. The technique proceeds in this way:

- The client is relaxed on a comfortable chair or couch in an office environment in which there are few distractions (e.g. bright lights, sounds). The client closes his/her eyes.
- The lowest item on the hierarchy is described and the client is instructed to imagine it, signalling (e.g. by raising an index finger) when the image is clear and vivid.
- The client is instructed to continue to imagine the scene for a brief period (typically 10–60 seconds), and is then told to stop imagining it and to focus once again on relaxing.
- After termination of the fantasy, the client signals whether the image had provoked anxiety (e.g. by raising the index finger of the other hand or by some other prearranged signal).
- The client continues to relax for a further minute or two and the

next scene is introduced; if the previous scene failed to elicit anxiety, and has failed to do so on three consecutive occasions, the next (more anxiety-provoking) item on the hierarchy is introduced.

The procedure continues for about 30–40 minutes, moving up the hierarchy as indicated above.

The counsellor seeks feedback from the client concerning difficulty conjuring up a scene, or why it is that certain scenes produce a persistent anxiety response. Difficulty in producing an image sometimes indicates that it is too threatening and the procedure should revert to a lower or newly devised item. When the scene is imagined it may change in unexpected ways and unrecognized threatening aspects may come to the fore. The hierarchy/hierarchies may need to be reformulated in the light of this feedback.

Progress is monitored by re-rating hierarchy items on 0–10 or 0–100 scales of subjective disturbance. Progression through several hierarchies normally takes 20–40 sessions, whereas alternate methods typically achieve similar results in 5–20 sessions. A generalization of anxiety reduction from imaginary to real-life situations does not always occur automatically, but clients are normally instructed to engage in homework tasks to ensure this, with the counsellor taking care not to suggest difficult tasks that would resensitize the client.

Covert rehearsal

The conclusion from later research findings was that more attention should be given to *what* a client imagines him/herself doing in the fantasy – for example, the extent to which the client imagines him/herself engaging the source of threat. Covert rehearsal refers to instructions to the client to imagine actively coping in the situation. Instructions to imagine coping with a realistic degree of difficulty are generally more effective than suggesting complete mastery. The technique can be combined with relaxation, as above, or with *applied relaxation*, that is, coping with the provocative scene by deliberately using a quick relaxation technique (see chapter 8).

The client reports back on the way the image develops, and the counsellor can use this information to suggest modifications to the fantasy in subsequent scenes. The aim is to assist the client to rehearse appropriate responses with minimal distress. Most clients know what the appropriate response is and have the skills to exercise it – the problem for them in real situations is that the defensive response is prepotent and prevents them acting adaptively. Clients are given homework assignments to consolidate fantasized rehearsal.

Flooding in fantasy

This is a technique to confront the client with anxiety-provoking images for a period of 40–60 minutes. The counsellor describes scenes in vivid and concrete detail, the relevant content having been established beforehand. The scene can include material to provoke unusual perceptual experiences which cannot otherwise be elicited, or can include elements that have no basis in reality (e.g. witnessing others' reactions to one's own death). The relevance of the material is confirmed by the client although the counsellor may have to embroider it during the fantasy in a creative manner. An example is given in the following section.

Extract from a flooding in fantasy script

This fantasy was devised for a man who occasionally experienced 'sleep paralysis', a short-lived, infrequent and harmless phenomenon which for him had become quite terrifying. The fear was discovered by the counsellor when the client was given instructions for relaxation and was found to be unable to close his eyes. Themes for the fantasy were identified beforehand and ad-libbed for a period of 40 minutes; anxiety ratings were obtained at intervals and showed a consistent decline within and across sessions:

> 'You are just waking up in the morning. You are about to move your arm but your arm is paralysed. You have no control over your arm or any other part of your body. You are paralysed. Your mind is active and alert and you begin to feel panicky as you fully realize that you can't move. You try to call out to your wife. Nothing, not even a strangled cry, escapes your lips. You panic even more now, your heart is pounding and sweat is dripping from your face. No one can reach you, no one can help you. You imagine yourself lost for ever, like being lost in space from your spacecraft, drifting hopelessly, out of touch with all humanity, with no hope of return. Space and emptiness around you, a no man's land of non-existence. A feeling of complete isolation envelops you and your panic intensifies. You feel you can't take any more of the panic, so many sensations from your body piercing your consciousness [etc etc.].'

The client gives a rating of distress at intervals so that the effect of the fantasy can be monitored. The same anxiety-provoking imagery is repeated until it ceases to be upsetting. A fantasy may have to be continued for at least 20–30 minutes before distress is reduced. A 40-minute session is therefore the minimum duration that is advisable.

When this method was first introduced it was considered important from a theoretical point of view to use material representing the ultimate threats potentially posed by the situation. In some cases, even the worst conceivable threats were exaggerated – hence the name 'flooding'. There is a risk with such an approach of sensitizing the client, and in any case these recommendations may have little validity. This is not to suggest that significant dimensions of threat should be left out. Some means of incorporating them in a graded manner can usually be found. The method being advocated is therefore more accurately referred to as prolonged fantasy rather than flooding in fantasy, and earlier guidelines on grading the material can be followed.

One advantage of this technique is that bodily arousal evoked by the fantasy is experienced in a safe setting. Internal cues arising out of physiological processes are often perceived as threatening, quite apart from the fact that they are unpleasant. The counsellor should focus the client's attention on these cues and their significance during the fantasy.

Guided fantasy

This is a more prolonged fantasy evocation with fewer constraints and greater interplay between client and counsellor. Its use in assessment was illustrated earlier (chapter 5). The client is instructed to describe aloud, in the first-person present tense, a relevant episode of distress. Guidance of the fantasy takes the following form:

- Instruct the client to amplify on various aspects (events, bodily reactions etc.).
- Invite the client to respond to new elements (suppose X happens or Y is said, how are you reacting?). .
- Suggest rehearsing alternative ways of reacting, and noting the consequences.
- The counsellor engages more fully by acting a part to which the client responds imaginatively.

The purpose of guided fantasy, used therapeutically, is to help the client uncover and confront threatening elements and rehearse appropriate responses. It is also an opportunity for the counsellor to engage the client in cognitively restructuring the experience (see chapter 7).

The length of a guided fantasy is, typically, 15–60 minutes. The counselling process can move in and out of the fantasy mode as issues are exposed, feedback provided, explanation and instruction given, and so forth.

Self-managed confrontation
For certain anxiety problems such as fear of public places or social fears, a programme of self-managed confrontation is the preferred approach because confrontation takes place normally and inevitably between sessions. Time within sessions can be diverted to devising suitable homework tasks and also to supplementary methods of behavioural rehearsal or imaginal confrontation. Detailed guidelines are given in chapter 7.

Suggestions for further reading

The theoretical basis of confrontational methods has been discussed by Barlow (1988: chapter 8), Foa and Kozak (1986), Goldfried (1986), Watts (1979), Williams (1990) and Wilson (1986).

7

Panic Attack and Associated Phobias

Onset and description of panic

The origin of a large proportion of anxiety problems can be traced back to unpleasant episodes of altered sensation and feeling which may have lasted no longer than a few minutes. The cause of these episodes is still largely a mystery although it is known that many of them arise in the context of prolonged stress. Stressors commonly reported at the onset are death or illness of relatives, illness in self, interpersonal conflict, and changes in consciousness induced by anaesthesia or mind-altering drugs.

The nature of the initial episodes is extremely variable from one person to another. They are not always described as instances of anxiety and panic – in fact, it is more likely that the episode will be attributed to physical or mental illness. It is not yet known whether all of the first reports of anomalous experience *are*, in fact, expressions of 'anxiety'; they may well become so as a result of being perceived as signifying some sort of threat. In some cases, however, the first episode is one of unbidden and inexplicable terror or panic. In other cases, the onset takes a gradual, incremental course, with each episode (spaced by days, weeks or months) acquiring greater intensity and experienced as more fearful. Some clients continue to believe that they are physically ill and this attribution may be hard to shift. Typical presentations of the problem are shown in Table 7.1.

The following quotations illustrate clients' descriptions of the first episodes.

Client A
I was walking up the road when I started to feel sort of dizzy. I thought 'What's happening?' I had experienced palpitations before but nothing to this extent. I thought I'd keep on walking but it got worse; my legs started to go; I felt in every part of me there was something wrong; I couldn't breathe; I was constantly swallowing; my throat seemed to close up and I felt like screaming out 'somebody help'.

Table 7.1 *Ways in which panic is first revealed as a problem*

1 A series of episodes of anomalous sensation, initially of a minor sort and not necessarily regarded as 'anxiety', but later escalating in severity in terms of their frightening nature.

2 An unexpected full-blown 'panic attack' accompanied by intense somatic sensations and an urge to flee.

3 Complaints of a somatic kind presented to a physician (e.g. relating to the heart, dizziness, chest pain, breathing difficulty, problem in swallowing, weakness, stomach upset).

4 Dependence on or abuse of alcohol or any other chemical form of sedation or tranquillization. The 'anxiety problem' is masked or is revealed only when an attempt is made to withdraw the substance.

5 A feeling that the world is unreal (derealization) or that the self is unreal and lacking in spontaneity (depersonalization). This may occur initially as a minor episode or be associated with an initial major episode.

Client B
Well I was feeling quite normal, driving along this road I knew well when, for no apparent reason, I noticed I was high up. There and then I felt as if a shudder went right through me. I ignored it and didn't give it another thought. Two weeks later, on the same road, the same thing happened. In fact before I got to the high part, I was aware of it and as soon as I got on to it proper, it was even worse than before. So I asked myself 'What is this?' I didn't mention it to anyone, thinking it would go away.

Client C
I was crossing the road and, when I got to the middle part, with nothing around me, I suddenly panicked. I was aware of all the space around me, nothing I could touch. I went sort of clammy and nervous, I could feel my heart beating, and I had to run to the other side and hold on to a lamp-post. A few months later the same thing happened; then it often happened crossing roads, crossing parks. I found I couldn't walk down steps, at least not in the middle of them. I had to hold on to the banister and go very slowly. If I looked down I felt dizzy, and I thought I was going to fall. Sometimes it was easier to turn around and actually crawl down them backwards.

The situation in which the initial episode occurs is usually mildly stressful and some degree of entrapment is often present. Examples of initial situations are travelling by bus or underground train, walking over a high bridge, or crossing a road. However, in many instances the situation appears to be non-stressful. Waking in the night in terror is a not infrequent mode of onset in which case the person may fear falling asleep.

Clients are likely to report several of the somatic sensations listed in Table 5.2 (p. 52). The episode itself may last from a few minutes up to an hour, but 10–15 minutes is typical. Some clients have a notion of what awful catastrophe might happen to them during the panic. Some common catastrophic interpretations are listed below. Other clients simply refer to groundless fears or unpleasant bodily sensations. When catastrophic fears are not overtly expressed, it may take a considerable length of time to reach the point where the client is able to articulate them. Links with past traumatic events including physical or sexual abuse are occasionally uncovered, leading into other areas of counselling. In some cases there appear to be no catastrophic thoughts associated with panic.

Some common catastrophic interpretations of behaviours, feelings and sensations associated with panic

Die	Lose one's memory
Faint	Lose touch with reality
Collapse	Scream out loud
Become physically ill	Strike out and hit someone
Have a heart attack	Give in to an impulse to commit suicide
Suffer a brain tumour or stroke	Suffer unbearably
Lose control of bladder or bowels	Cause a scene
Have a nervous breakdown	Humiliate oneself in front of others
Become insane	Make a fool of oneself
Become paralysed	Unable to function (work, etc.)
Become hysterical	Partner/spouse will leave

Consequences of panic

Panic-like episodes occur very commonly in the general population and so the most likely outcome is that they pass off inconsequentially. In a minority of cases they represent the starting point of an escalating anxiety problem. As far as the counsellor is concerned, at least a half of anxiety problems will be observed to have started in this way. What occurs typically is that the client dreads having another 'attack' and at the same time becomes extremely concerned about the meaning of the episode. Several consequences follow:

There is *greater awareness of, and dependence on, safety cues* such as the physical presence of another person, reassurance by telephone contact, or the safety of familiar places (e.g. home or car). Some examples of safety cues are listed below. There is a tendency, resisted by some clients, to avoid places of relative danger in which it is anticipated that panic is more likely to occur. Episodes are less likely to happen in 'safe' environments but their absence can never be fully guaranteed. If the client gives in to the urge to avoid risky situations, a cluster of phobias of public places develops which has been given the psychiatric label of agoraphobia or the agoraphobic syndrome. This term, meaning a fear of public places, is a misnomer because what is feared is the possibility of panicking in these places, not the places themselves.

Safety cues – situations that tend to decrease the risk of panic
Being with a trusted companion
Sitting or standing close to door or exit
Walking close to physical supports (e.g. walls)
Access to telephone or other source of help
Holding, carrying, pushing something (e.g. umbrella, shopping trolley, bag)
Company of a pet animal
Wearing sunglasses
Wearing talisman (e.g. St Christopher medallion)
Carrying tranquillizer

The phobia that develops may be quite circumscribed, especially if the initial episodes have occurred under clearly defined circumstances such as an enclosed place or a high place. In fact, the type of phobia arising out of panic may depend on a fortuitous connection between the panic episode and the sort of situation in which it occurs. Not all circumscribed phobias start in this way, however.

There is *increased vigilance* for signs of an impending 'attack'. The episodes are partly predictable on the basis of situational or internal (mental/bodily) cues. Situational cues that are commonly associated with an increased likelihood of panic are given in Table 7.2. Crowded places are disliked, not so much because they involve social interaction, but because a crowd blocks escape. Being observed by another person, especially when panicking, may heighten embarrassment and lead to fears of appearing ridiculous or insane. Risky situations tend to be places which would be mildly stressful to anyone (bright lights, loud sounds, high places, darkness, close physical presence of others) or places that constrain escape or the freedom to act in a general sense (e.g. sitting in the middle of a row, sitting in a hairdresser's chair). Clients may feel constrained by fixed appointments, such as visits to friends, or

Table 7.2 Situations that tend to increase the risk of panic

Situation	*Probable stimulus features: VS	RE	N	AH	P	GS	SE	H	C
Increasing distance from home or car		✓							
Unfamiliar surroundings			✓						
Wide, high, open spaces	✓		✓						
Narrow, enclosed spaces	✓								
High places	✓	✓							
Being close to edge of platform, parapet etc.		✓							
Waiting in a queue (e.g. bus stop, checkout)		✓							
Having a haircut		✓						✓	✓
Crowded places		✓						✓	✓
Making an appointment				✓					
Being alone				✓					
Hot weather, bright sunlight	✓				✓				
Dull or wintry weather									
Darkness				✓					
Tiredness, low mood					✓	✓			
Physical illness					✓	✓		✓	
Physical exercise					✓	✓			
Caffeine (tea and coffee)					✓	✓			
Thinking over problems					✓	✓			
Domestic arguments						✓		✓	
Being observed by others (e.g. across room, in a train)		✓					✓	✓	✓
Perceived as inferior, subordinate etc.						✓	✓		

*VS = visuo-spatial; RE = restricted escape route; N = novelty; AH = absence of help/reassurance; P = physiological factors; GS = general stressors; SE = social evaluation; H = possibility of harm to self; C = close physical presence of others attending an occasion such as a wedding. These occasions are normally pleasurable if there is no anticipatory period and the opportunity to attend is 'sprung' on the person. The concern underlying fixed appointments appears to be that the freedom to decline the invitation has been lost and that the client might feel constrained to attend while feeling panicky.

A heightened vigilance for situational cues may lead to increased precautionary action and a broadening of the number of situations that are avoided. The problem becomes more and more limiting with an inevitable loss of opportunities for work, travel, leisure, and personal relationships. Intimate and family relationships may suffer and a depressed mood may result.

The *internal* cues that can act as warning signs fall into two groups – mental and bodily. The person develops a vigilant, self-observing attitude, often accompanied by checking for 'symptoms'. He/she might arrange a series of appointments with members of the medical profession in the hope of gaining reassurance that a symptom is not 'serious'. If the initial episodes took place in the context of alterations in consciousness (e.g. feeling unreal) greater vigilance may be directed to mental signs such as memory lapses, confusion or a return of feelings of unreality.

In a typical client, the perceived risk of panicking is related to subtle aspects of mood and confidence on a particular day. Clients seem to know whether a day is going to be 'good' or 'bad' for them. The source of evidence for this conviction is often obscure (e.g. 'shakiness') but is probably well founded. The tendency to panic can fluctuate markedly: some clients remain free of any sign of distress for weeks, months or even years. However, once established, the tendency to panic usually remains, often for decades, unless effective help is obtained.

Some women report that they are more vulnerable to panic when they are pre-menstrual. Depressed mood and stressful interpersonal interaction can sometimes be identified as influential. A client's theory about what is significant can and should be checked out through diary monitoring of episodes. The pattern of episodes may turn out to be related to physiological factors that could be corrected. All clients should have been screened first by a physician but referral becomes imperative when diary monitoring reveals anomalous mental or bodily signs that seem to bear no relationship at all to psychological or environmental factors.

Other internal cues about which the client becomes vigilant are bodily sensations such as irregular or rapid heartbeats, tingling sensations, unsteadiness, light-headedness, blurred vision, and many more. These bodily sensations may have been experienced in association with past 'attacks' but are now attended to as signs of an impending 'attack'. The predictive value of these bodily sensations is uncertain given that they can accompany a variety of innocuous happenings such as physical exercise, emotional excitement, drinking strong coffee, colds, flu and gastric upsets. They are also present in normal everyday situations that are stressful or anxiety provoking. Through association with extremely distressing episodes in the past, a person may come to view the bodily sensation as a sign that another such episode is pending. The perception of threat mediates increased autonomic nervous system (ANS) arousal thereby increasing the evidence that the prediction will be confirmed. In this way, vigilance about bodily sensations, far from helping to ward off further episodes, may actually precipitate them. In some circumstances, attention to bodily sensations sets the occasion for withdrawal to a safer environment or acts as a cue for the use of pills or alcohol. Consequently, the threat attaching to the bodily sensation remains undiminished; any opportunity to learn that the sensation is *not* followed by dire consequences is lost through avoidance.

The importance of bodily sensations as cues for episodes of anxiety and panic has now been fully recognized by clinical researchers and interventions have been devised to break their connection with threat (see p. 98).

A reliance on chemical calming agents may develop as a result of efforts to manage panic episodes. Alcohol is extremely effective in the short term for subduing an anxious frame of mind and some people become addicted to it in this way. Questioning clients about use of alcohol should be routine. As soon as the effect of alcohol wears off, clients typically report feeling *more* 'shaky' and vulnerable to anxiety. This sequence of events, if remedied by further resort to alcohol, can lead rapidly to dependence.

The same process is generally true of tranquillizing medication. There is a tendency towards dependence as tolerance of the drug develops. A larger dose is needed to produce the same effect. Withdrawal from a drug can lead to a return of anxiety complaints as well as some new effects such as insomnia and vivid, unpleasant dreams (see chapter 9). For this reason, where clients are taking tranquillizing medication regularly, it is important that the pills are taken at evenly spaced intervals to avoid a see-sawing effect (this is not of concern with irregular use of single doses for specific purposes).

Assessment of panic and associated phobias

The initial interviews should aim to elicit the features of the problem outlined above. Descriptions of recent panic episodes are likely to be most informative but a client may not have attended to features (such as accompanying thoughts) that need to be assessed. For this purpose, anxiety should be evoked and observed in the presence of the counsellor. The process of assessment merges into educating the client and modifying thoughts and images. In other words, the client's thoughts and behaviour, as reported in descriptions of recent incidents or observed by the counsellor, are the material on which client and counsellor work.

There are clear advantages in being systematic about recording the nature, frequency and severity of episodes. Progress, even though slow and steady, may not be immediately noticeable to a client. Moreover, when clients' sights are set on being completely free of their problem, they tend to discount even the obvious changes they have made in their behaviour. Diary monitoring of episodes is one way of demonstrating that progress has occurred. The results can be graphed if desired. Some clients make such rapid progress that no demonstration of this fact is required. For a significant proportion, however, especially clients struggling with other problems or disadvantages, counselling is likely to be extended, in some difficult cases over several years. A record of progress helps to motivate a client to persist. What is important is the overall trend, and clients should be informed that progress is likely to be irregular, with repeated setbacks. When a setback occurs, a counsellor may be able to show that it is of lesser significance than previous setbacks the client has recorded in the diary, or that in relation to the magnitude of previous difficulties this setback is likely to be one that the client can overcome.

Progress is revealed through changes in:

- the extent and degree of avoidance of situations (bearing in mind that clients may be relying initially on safety cues to enter situations, and that some clients show minimal avoidance);
- ratings of the severity of distress in situations;
- the frequency of panic and anxiety episodes.

A record of the type shown in Table 7.3 is useful for assessing change over long intervals but weekly progress is best assessed by means of a diary that records responses to both planned events (homework tasks) and other unplanned but relevant day-to-day activities. The diary should indicate accomplishments as well as

Table 7.3 *Severity and extent of situational avoidance*

Avoidance rating – none; slight avoidance; usually avoid; always avoid
Expected severity of distress – 0 = none; 10 = as anxious, panicky, distressed as I have ever been.

The situations listed are those that the client expects to enter without anxiety and are particularly relevant to the client's goals.

Example	Avoidance	Expected severity of distress
Driving to mother's home	None	2
Driving to local supermarket	None	2
Having coffee with neighbour	Slight	3
Inviting own family to dinner	Slight	3
Shopping in local supermarket	None	4
Going out to dinner at friend's house	Slight	4
Walking to local supermarket	Usually	6
Taking bus to local supermarket	Always	6
Going to restaurant with partner	Usually	6
Spending 10 minutes in local shopping centre alone	Slight	6
Spending 1 hour in local shopping centre with partner	Slight	6
Spending 1 hour in local shopping centre alone	Always	10
Going away for weekend with partner by car (more than 50 miles)	Always	10
Flying abroad for holiday with partner	Always	10

problem situations, giving the counsellor an opportunity to comment on or praise the client for the successful attainment of goals. Overall progress is indicated by confronting new situations (previously avoided), and by decrease in ratings of distress in situations regularly entered (e.g. a particular supermarket, eating in a restaurant). A suitable diary format is given in Table 7.4. The diary should not be too onerous to complete. A simple record well kept is better than a complex one that is not kept at all. Clients should be encouraged to improve the accuracy and completeness of their records, for example by recording soon after an event, and certainly on the same day. The client might find it most convenient to carry a small notebook and pen. The meaning of the anchor points on rating scales should be discussed and, if discrete panic episodes are to be recorded, how they should be defined (e.g. by length, severity of episode, or type of sensation). The frequency of episodes is not necessarily an accurate indicator of progress because it depends on the number of situations confronted. The

Table 7.4   *Diary record of anxiety and panic*

Simple Record

Date	Activity and situation	Time spent in activity	Highest rating (0–10)	Comment (e.g. consequences, thoughts)

Complex Record

Additional columns can be added as follows:
   Time activity started
   Time activity ended
   Performed alone or with others
   Distress rating at beginning and end of activity
   Accompanying negative thoughts
   Coping strategies (e.g. distraction, medication)
   Details of panic attacks (duration, intensity, and antecedents, associated
   mental and physical signs)

frequency and severity of panic episodes that are unexpected and apparently unrelated to situational cues may have greater validity in this respect.

The complex record (see Table 7.4) gives more precise information about the timing of activities, the time course of the diminution of distress, the precise nature of the panic episode, and use of coping strategies. This information should not be sought unless there is good reason. For example, the counsellor might be interested in breathing difficulties and use of slow breathing strategies, implementation of applied relaxation, identification of irrational thoughts, and so on. A short discussion of the diary entries should be scheduled for the beginning of a session. The way the information is used is indicated on p. 104.

Additional guidelines in applying confrontation methods

These guidelines supplement those in chapter 6 and are necessary to take account of the special features of this class of anxiety problem. These are:

- the multiple, ubiquitous stimulus conditions that may trigger the problems. Clients can achieve only relative safety from panic episodes. Panic may occur without obvious triggering events and therefore the problem pervades almost all aspects of the client's life.
- the importance of internal cues such as bodily sensations, mental images, and frightening thoughts. By their very nature, these cues are inescapable although distraction and deliberate thought-suppression are sometimes partially effective in limiting their effect.
- the way in which a client's associates are drawn into the problem through carrying out tasks for the client or accompanying him or her or providing reassurance.

The implications of these three features are, first, that the stimulus antecedents are not readily controllable, reproducible or even identifiable and, second, that the consequences of the problem on the client's life often exacerbate and complicate matters. Modifying the response to cues for panic is clearly a central objective. In other words, a client is shown methods through which the intensity of the episode can be lessened and shown ways of preventing the episodes from escalating. The essential steps are as follows:

1 Identify cues for panic.
2 Elicit these cues under controlled circumstances.
3 Neutralize the threat associated with the cues by:
   - familiarity through prolonged confrontation;
   - substituting neutral/innocuous interpretations for threatening ones;
   - helping the client to acquire control over internal cues that are interpreted as threatening.

Methods for identifying cues and triggers for panic were discussed earlier. A cue such as walking in the street may be obvious but more precise triggers in this situation can be elusive. In the absence of this knowledge, methods such as prolonged confrontation can still be employed effectively. Guidelines for this approach will be given later, following a discussion of internal cues

Table 7.5 *Sensations commonly associated with over-breathing*

- Pins and needles (tingling sensations usually at the extremity of the limbs)
- Numbness in parts of the body
- Feeling faint, lightheaded or dizzy
- Hot and cold flushes
- Strong heartbeats or racing heart
- Feeling shaky/unsteady
- Weak legs
- Visual disturbances
- Lump in the throat

arising from over-breathing and sensitivity to space and motion stimuli.

Internal cues arising out of over-breathing (hyperventilation)

When a person exercises or gets emotionally excited, there is an increase in the rate and depth of breathing. The physiological requirement for oxygen increases under these conditions and this is satisfied by increasing the flow of air through the lungs. Besides a change in rate and depth of breathing, there is a tendency to switch from breathing with the diaphragm (indicated by raising and lowering of the stomach) to breathing by raising the shoulders and expanding the chest (thoracic breathing). Hyperventilation refers to a pattern of breathing yielding an *excess* of oxygen in the lungs, above requirements. The raised oxygen results in removal of carbon dioxide from the blood so that the blood becomes more alkaline. This has the effect of causing certain bodily sensations which are harmless but may be experienced as unpleasant. The drop of carbon dioxide in the blood is automatically sensed by the brain which sends messages to shut down the rate of breathing. Subjectively, this may be experienced as an inability to breathe or as difficulty in breathing. There might be a sensation of feeling short of air, followed by a forced attempt at breathing; the chest might feel tight as well.

The relevance of hyperventilation is suggested when clients particularly mention their breathing and describe a number of the sensations in Table 7.5. (It should be noted that the sensations listed can arise for other reasons as well.)

Tingling and lightheadedness can be present much of the time, even in the absence of complaints of difficulty in breathing or of anxiety. The cluster of signs of hyperventilation are sometimes produced by light exercise (e.g. climbing stairs). Observation of the client at interview or during behavioural test can reveal irregular or sighing respiration or thoracic breathing. Direct measurement of carbon dioxide levels in the blood can be done but this facility is not usually available. As a diagnostic test, a client can be asked to over-breathe for two minutes in order to find out whether the sensations produced in this way are similar to, or provoke, an episode of panic. No precise figure can be given of the proportion of clients in whom hyperventilation plays a role but some researchers imply that it is very high.

It is explained to the client that over-breathing is responsible for some anxiety problems and that a test for hyperventilation would help to establish whether this is true in the client's case. The client is warned that the test might produce some mildly unpleasant sensations (without being too specific) but that these are harmless. The test should ideally run for its full length but the option to terminate it earlier (or refuse it altogether) is given.

Instructions for hyperventilation test   (NB: it is inadvisable to carry out this test on clients who have medical disorders of the cardiovascular or respiratory systems, emphysema, bronchitis, epilepsy, metabolic/hormonal disorder, or any serious physical disorder, or who are pregnant.) The sensations produced by the test can be removed quickly by instructing the client to rebreathe their own air using a *paper* bag held firmly around nose and mouth. (The counsellor can demonstrate this and have a bag available.)

1 The client reports any sensations they are experiencing *before* the test.
2 While remaining in the sitting position, the client breathes quickly for two minutes through the nose and mouth, fully expelling air in each breath. The counsellor first demonstrates at a rate of approximately 30 breaths per minute (the normal rate is 8–12 breaths).
3 The client is encouraged to continue and is prompted to do it as instructed.
4 The client stops when the two minutes have elapsed (or before) and reports on the sensations they are experiencing. (Asking the client to stand up may elicit further sensations.)

The sensations are noted down together with any behavioural observations during the test. The length of time the client maintains over-breathing is recorded. If the sensations remain for more than a few minutes, the client can be asked to use the paper bag for one or two minutes or to slow down their breathing by pausing after each breath out.

The importance of hyperventilation is suggested when the client reacts with strong emotion and can see the similarity with sensations experienced during panic episodes. Because the test occurs in a safe environment, a client may note the similarity without being unduly distressed. The effects of over-breathing can be used as evidence to dispute a client's negative interpretation of sensations which are now seen to have a natural explanation. The strategies a counsellor can use to help the client reattribute the cause of sensations to hyperventilation are described below.

Intervention strategies for hyperventilation When there is a definite similarity between the sensations experienced during panic and during the test of hyperventilation (and other indications of over-breathing are also present), it may benefit the client to focus efforts on changing the breathing pattern. Hyperventilation may be a contributory if not the main trigger for panic.

1 Reattribution. The purpose here is to convince the client that sensations associated with panic are attributable to hyperventilation rather than a more threatening cause. The hyperventilation test may not be convincing, however, if the client does not over-breathe for long enough or feels safe in the counsellor's presence. Doubts the client may have can be answered by questioning the client about the likely effect of over-breathing for longer, while alone in a fearful situation, and so on.

Clients should be informed that the rate of breathing increases during anxiety even though a person may not be aware of this fact. Attention can be drawn to the *first* sensations experienced during panic and whether these could be explained by over-breathing. As in cognitive restructuring generally (see p. 110), the counsellor avoids lecturing the client and instead leads by questions that allow the client to come to his/her own conclusion. However, an ability on the counsellor's part to explain previously inexplicable phenomena is also convincing. For example, chest pain can be explained as a result of prolonged over-breathing when the lungs are already relatively full (i.e. the expanded intercostal muscles begin to tighten in response to over-breathing). The physical effort and fatiguing effect of over-breathing can be pointed out.

2 Training in slow diaphragmatic breathing. The purpose here is twofold: first, to train clients in a technique they can apply when anxious and over-breathing; second, to train a style of breathing that is less effortful and more conducive to relaxation generally (see chapter 8). Breathing is not normally a process to which attention is given. In fact, clients who become self-conscious about it may find it harder to achieve a slow regular rhythm. Simple instructions such as the following may be sufficient to regularize the rate when a client is anxious or panicking: 'Just remember to relax your shoulders when breathing out all the air. Then pause for a while or count up to three. Don't worry about breathing in – that will take care of itself.'

This technique can be practised during relaxation training, at first with the counsellor, and then at home with audio-recorded relaxation instructions and suggestions for slowing down breathing in the manner indicated. Relaxation tapes are available commercially but they are unlikely to contain sufficiently detailed instructions for breathing. I use a sequence of suggestions which I have recorded personally and then copy for the client. (The recording should ideally be made with high-quality equipment in a sound-proofed room; see chapter 8 for guidelines on content.)

When slow breathing is taught as a coping technique, the client rehearses a sequence of over-breathing for 15 seconds followed by a breathing control manoeuvre (slowed breathing or rebreathing with paper bag). In order to apply the technique and generalize its use, a counsellor can prompt the client to employ the technique during anxiety-provoking confrontations with real or imagined situations.

Some experts advocate regular home practice with a respiratory pacing audio tape. This has prolonged articulations of the words 'in' and 'out' repeated at a rate which is several breaths per minute slower than the client's resting rate of breathing. The aim is to attain, in stages, a rate of 8–10 breaths a minute. The voice prompt is eventually faded out as paced breathing comes under voluntary control.

Internal cues arising out of disequilibrium and dizziness
The maintenance of balance is a complex, taken-for-granted and largely automatic bodily function. Balance is controlled by multiple sources of sensory information which are integrated in the brain, where instructions are given for motor adjustments and righting reflexes. The main sensory systems contributing to balance are vision, inner ear (vestibular) balance organs, touch, pressure and muscle receptors, and joint receptors in the cervical spine. If one sense is dysfunctional or damaged, compensatory adjustments can be made centrally and greater reliance may be placed on alternative sensory channels.

The vestibular-ocular reflexes are involved in maintaining a stable visual world as the body moves about in relation to it. The sensation of (true) vertigo is a sense of the world (or self) *spinning*, familiar to anyone who has drunk too much alcohol. This is a symptom of visuo-spatial disorientation in which the maintenance of a stable visual world breaks down under conditions of incongruous sensory input or physical disorder of the underlying mechanisms. Vertigo should be distinguished from lightheadedness, giddiness or faintness, in which spinning sensations are absent. In fact, the 'dizziness' reported by anxious clients is rarely true vertigo.

However, disturbances of balance (including vertigo) commonly lead to complaints of anxiety and fears of public places. It is not surprising that an episode of vertigo should give rise to fear, given that it may be accompanied by a fall to the ground, nausea, vomiting and a general sense of fatigue and incapacitation after the episode. A person might understandably develop a fear of losing control whilst driving or of becoming ill in embarrassing circumstances.

Some physical disorders that give rise to dizziness and imbalance (such as viral infections), produce symptoms that eventually remit, even though some objective evidence of dysfunction remains. In other cases, such as Ménières disorder or certain central dysfunctions, symptoms of dizziness and imbalance can persist intermittently or recur under conditions of impoverished or incongruous sensory input.

It is still being debated whether psychological factors can be a primary cause of true dizziness and of imbalance. In some individuals, the 'symptoms' appear in stressful or emotional circumstances. In whatever way the physical and psychological factors interact, there appears to be a sub-group of clients with anxiety problems who are particularly affected by *space and motion stimuli* or respond to stressors with dizziness/imbalance. 'Space phobia' involves fear of falling when no support is at hand and there are few visual cues for orientation. Some clients may be discomforted or made anxious by zig-zag lines, moving lights, or alternating light and dark stripes. True vertigo may be absent but the client may report vaguer sensations of rocking, swaying or veering to one side or another.

Clients suspected of having disorders of the equilibrial sense should be referred to physicians but investigation may prove inconclusive. Discomfort experienced in the situations listed in Table 7.6 is suggestive of sensitivity to space and motion stimuli. These may be situations in which anxiety or panic is reported.

Table 7.6 *Situations in which a sensitivity to space and motion stimuli may be revealed*

Few visual stimuli suitable for orientation
  open field or open road
  darkness

Vestibular stimulation
  cornering or changing speed in car (especially as passenger)
  funfair rides
  head shaking
  elevators

Incongruous or complex space and motion cues
  looking out of the window of a car
  looking at wide-screen films
  looking at moving striped patterns
  observing lights in a tunnel while travelling through it
  walking down a stationary escalator
  looking at items on supermarket shelves
  passenger on boat at sea

Clients who show these sensitivities are not necessarily suffering from a medical disorder. The sensitivity can arise through loss of confidence in balance or inappropriate methods of using information to maintain balance.

Intervention strategies for space and motion sensitivity When clients have objective evidence of a balance disorder or chronic medical condition that produces symptoms of dizziness/imbalance, it is advisable to consult with the client's physician before embarking on any of the following strategies.

1 Education and reattribution. The relevance of space/motion cues is likely to become evident in discussion of the client's anxiety/panic diary. The client should be educated about the role of these cues in producing anomalous sensations and imbalance. These may have been wrongly attributed to mental illness by the client. Identifying and labelling them in neutral terms helps to decatastrophize them.

2 Vestibular habituation. Where the trigger appears to be vestibular stimulation (e.g. acceleration, deceleration, rotation), dizzy sensations can be deliberately provoked in a systematic and graded way. This might involve movements of the head (of greater or lesser vigour and duration in the orientation provoking dizziness), or physical exercises/sporting activities that involve grosser movements of the body. Acceleratory and deceleratory rotations on a swivel office chair can be employed as an easily controlled stimulus. The general rule to follow is that each stimulation of dizzy sensations should be followed by an adequate recovery period before proceeding to the next stimulation. (Duration of post-rotatory dizziness should become shorter with standard repetitions.)

3 Confrontation. Clients who feel insecure in the absence of nearby physical supports (e.g. crossing a road, standing on a wall) are normally able to become fully confident through graded confrontation. There may be fears of falling or collapsing that can be shown to be unfounded. Clients who are excessively reliant on the visual sense in order to feel orientated can be encouraged to rely on interoceptive mechanisms (e.g. by deflecting the gaze elsewhere, or balancing without vision).

Visual fixation on a stationary point is a useful strategy for suppressing spinning sensations.

Other internal cues associated with panic and anxiety

Any bodily cue associated with physical or emotional stressors may be perceived as an early sign of some catastrophic outcome or imminent panic. Some bodily sensations increase in intensity when they are given full attention. For example, heart pounding or sweating are likely to increase if a person attends to them, feels threatened and then responds anxiously. Other bodily sensations which are perceived as threatening (e.g. tinnitus, *petit mal* fits) do not escalate in the same manner because they are not usually intensified by activity of the autonomic nervous system.

In all cases where anxiety is cued by internal sensations, the principle to follow is to devise graded exercises that expose the client to the cue in safe circumstances. For some clients, the threat signified by a sensation is that of a serious physical illness or an anxiety about health in general. A fear of illness introduces new complexities into counselling, so this subject is discussed separately at the end of this chapter.

Self-managed confrontation

When cognitive-behavioural interventions were first developed for fears of public places, it was common for counsellors to accompany their clients into previously avoided situations. Although the counsellor's presence can be advantageous, the emphasis has now

switched to influencing the cognitive component of panic. Irrational thinking is revealed in the course of diary monitoring of
episodes or in response to exercises carried out in the counsellor's
office. The avoidance component of the problem is managed by
asking the client to carry out planned homework assignments. The
purpose of the assignment is to extend gradually the boundaries of
the territory in which he/she feels comfortable.

This shift in emphasis from real-life exercises to office-based
methods has occurred for various reasons:

- Clients are being seen who minimally avoid situations (despite
  their panic attacks) or they are being referred earlier after the
  initial episodes, before avoidance has developed. Panic attacks
  are therefore the most prominent feature of the problem.
- Research has shown that self-managed confrontation produces
  results comparable to that achieved by interventions in which the
  counsellor is also present during confrontation.
- It is now recognized that response to interoceptive cues and irrational beliefs plays a large part in vicious cycle phenomena.
  These components can be modified through office-based techniques.

There is now greater appreciation of the fact that effective
counselling is not just a matter of eliminating avoidance. The client
can benefit from assistance in making broader changes to his/her
lifestyle. For example, the elimination of avoidance may bring to
the fore problems in relationships, in being assertive, or starting up
new leisure interests.

As noted above, there are *some* advantages in having the
counsellor present when the client is confronting feared situations.
The counsellor can help the client to identify negative thoughts, to
cognitively restructure the situation, to analyse the task, to break
it down into manageable components, and to implement coping
strategies. When confrontation is self-managed, the guidelines need
to take account of this difference and also the absence of the
counsellor as a source of safety. The counsellor's job is to help the
client internalize the rules for grading homework tasks and mastering difficult situations. It is also important that the client avoid
situations likely to trigger overwhelmingly severe panic episodes
which could undermine motivation to continue. Guidelines for self-
managed confrontation are designed to minimize this possibility.
Advice is also given to help the client cope with the inevitable,
unexpected panic.

Aims and principles

The ultimate objective is for clients to engage in activities of their choice without concern that they will become excessively anxious or experience a severe panic attack. A client might have an unrealistic expectation that life should be free of all discomforting experiences, which is an irrational belief that might have to be countered during counselling. Clients should be led to expect that panic attacks *will* return unexpectedly although experience shows that these are likely to be of a lesser severity and occur at increasingly infrequent intervals. Some clients have only modest aims (e.g. to shop, take a holiday abroad, to eat out in a restaurant) in which case they will remain liable to experience anxiety when encountering more demanding situations. There is a risk that when significant sources of threat remain untackled, previous gains will be lost through a process of resensitization. The client should be made aware of this possibility.

The main aims of self-managed confrontation are to help the client:

- to understand the nature of anxiety and panic, when it is likely to occur, and how they can best respond to it. This aim is achieved through straightforward explanation, provision of reading material, and discussion of episodes recorded in a diary;
- to learn to tolerate and master unpleasant mental and bodily sensations. In the office, this may involve exercises to expose clients to specific interoceptive cues. Between sessions, clients confront situations that they would normally avoid, tolerate sensations of panic and anxiety, and through prolonged exposure and exercise of coping techniques gain confidence in mastering anxiety;
- to identify and counter irrational beliefs contributing to threat. The beliefs are identified in the course of analysing anxiety episodes recorded in a diary or otherwise occurring during office-based exercises. Countering beliefs takes the form of *task assignments* designed to test out a prediction arising out of a belief or *disputing a belief* through a Socratic style of questioning and reflection.

Guidelines for self-managed confrontation

Programmes follow the general guidelines for confrontation given in chapter 6 and progress is monitored by means of a diary record, as discussed earlier. The counsellor helps the client to plan daily activities and to overcome avoidance. Advice becomes most relevant at times of stress or when special events take place (such as family celebrations or holidays).

1 Cautious courage The client gradually internalizes rules for making judgements about when to tackle more difficult tasks, when to hold back rather than risk overwhelming anxiety, how to make situations easier through stepwise planning and anticipation of escape routes. The process of internalization occurs as clients discuss episodes of distress (and mastery) recorded in the diary. The application of the rules must be sufficiently flexible to take account of the fact that a client's confidence fluctuates from day to day. Although it is not always possible to discern a reason for this, the following factors may be important: mood; stressful life events; disappointments; and upcoming events which are anxiously anticipated.

Whenever possible, clients are encouraged to consolidate their routine achievements (such as going to the launderette) even if they feel disinclined to go on a particular day. Non-routine activities are given more forethought and can be timed flexibly. Some clients report exhaustion after confronting fear. Some seem to require a recovery period of a day or more after tackling a major task.

A client may attempt to 'fight' fear or 'break through the fear barrier' by tensing up and getting through a task as quickly as possible. This type of courage is misdirected; the aim is to face up to and accept the experience, notwithstanding the recommendation to use escape routes and 'crutches' (see p. 108) to give the client confidence in making the first step.

2 Planning and grading tasks Everyday activities contain variable options and potential outcomes. There is normally an opportunity to vary the elements and plan what to do in relation to different outcomes. For example in meeting someone for lunch there is the possibility of:

- meeting a trusted companion or a less intimate friend;
- meeting on familiar (e.g. home) or unfamiliar territory;
- if meeting out, examining possible meeting places in advance, with a view to noting how crowded they are at certain times of day, the layout of tables, etc;
- whether to explain to the companion the nature of the anxiety problem and what options the client intends to employ if difficulties arise;
- planning a spur-of-the moment invitation rather than a fixed appointment in order to avoid anxious anticipation;
- travelling by own car to increase flexibility rather than being dependent on public transport or a companion's car;
- choosing a table near to an exit or further inside;

- deciding the duration of the meeting or leaving it open;
- planning what to do in the event of a severe panic: e.g. leave to go to the toilet, leave to go and sit in the car and return when feeling calmer;
- deciding whether to use tranquillizing medication to make the task easier.

Even crossing a bridge can be broken down into small steps (look at it to size it up, walk part way and back, walk with a trusted companion, walk across to meet companion at the other end, drive across alone in a car, eventually walk across alone, at closer distances to the edge, and so on).

Discussion of anxiety incidents has the aim of helping the client internalize the following principles:

- the importance of repetition (regular practice). Clients should plan to confront anxiety-provoking situations at least several times a week;
- staying long enough for anxious feelings to subside;
- endeavouring to follow through with planned activities bearing in mind what was said under the heading 'Cautious courage' above;
- choosing new activities that are only somewhat more difficult than those already accomplished;
- being flexible about attaining goals, i.e. settling for partial completion rather than abandoning a task altogether;
- choosing meaningful activities for which there is some natural pay-off (e.g. making a purchase, meeting a friend, doing necessary domestic tasks, engaging in a sport or pastime);
- avoiding being trapped in situations (by the whim of others who change plans, being dependent on unreliable sources of help, etc.).

3 Use of 'crutches' A crutch can be defined as any device or support that allows a client to approach a difficult task with greater confidence and chance of success. The aim, however, is to discard the crutch as confidence increases. Normally this means:

- using companions and other safety cues;
- employing distraction (from anxious thoughts and situations);
- adopting fail-safe plans.

As suggestions for the use of distraction, clients can start a conversation or look attentively at objects in a shop window. One client wore a Walkman and played a recording of Claire Weekes giving her admirable mixture of advice, hope and reassurance to anxiety sufferers.

Tranquillizing medication can be helpful on one-off occasions. Medication is occasionally of value in the short term in the case of chronic insomnia although the longer-term aim is to achieve a normal sleep pattern by psychological means.

4 *Detached acceptance* As clients begin to accept the harmlessness of their sensations and understand their own fear reactions, they can usually be persuaded to take the stance of a curious detached observer to their own panic episodes. 'Accepting' a sensation means allowing oneself to experience it fully, as expressed by the notion of 'floating with anxiety'.

Tasks should be approached in a relaxed accepting manner, that is, the client should walk at a normal pace with a relaxed posture. If tensing up becomes obvious, the client should pause, perhaps sit down, or lean against a wall. It can be helpful for the client to jot down the sensations and thoughts they are having or to say to themselves: 'This is unpleasant but it will pass' or 'I know this is another panic – it won't hurt me.'

A client might hit upon some phrase or image that works especially well for them, such as: 'What the hell – if you're going to die, you're going to die' or 'I'll put myself in God's hands. His will be done, so why worry.' A helpful image might be that of successfully mastering a specific situation in the past.

As part of a strategy to encourage acceptance, it can be suggested to a client to admit the problem to others and explain it in simple terms. (Exceptions may have to be made in the case of work colleagues.) Resistance to this suggestion may reveal assumptions about the shamefulness of the problem which can be disputed.

5 *Using helpers* The counsellor should enquire into the availability of helpers to accompany the client when confronting difficult situations. Helpers are valuable to: encourage and motivate the client; act as a source of safety; distract the client from anxious thoughts.

The client should explain to helpers the principles of confrontation and the helper role in the client's programme. Guidance to helpers may be offered by the counsellor. A handout is helpful in this regard (See Appendix B). It should always be the client who is left with the decision about which task to tackle next. The partner of the client is not necessarily the most suitable helper, especially if the partner resents or overprotects the client, has a tendency to sneer at success, or becomes anxious on behalf of the client. These issues should be addressed in a joint session with the partner or family member if the client is unable to deal with them alone.

An ex-phobic or sympathetic friend is the ideal helper. Helpers should be reliable, trustworthy and non-judgemental. Helping should be regular and planned. It may be time consuming as prolonged sessions are better than brief ones. Local self-help organizations may be able to assist. Helping is a temporary phase in self-management of the problem and should eventually be faded out.

6 *Consolidating progress* Clients should be informed that confrontation must be repeated if progress is to be consolidated. Changing behaviour on one occasion is not sufficient to overcome an anxiety problem. Clients should be advised that they may become less confident when physically ill, depressed or stressed, and should adjust their activities accordingly. It may be difficult for a client to repeat a task if a panic episode has been followed by weeks of inactivity.

The counsellor reviews progress periodically by asking the client to re-rate the initial list of targets. Clients frequently forget or discount how much they have changed and a review of this kind can instil a sense of achievement and encourage new efforts.

As constraints on the client's behaviour are lifted, new opportunities arise, relationships change, and the increased sense of freedom may feel threatening. Counsellors should set aside time to help clients re-evaluate their lives.

The counsellor is likely to fade out slowly rather than terminate sessions abruptly. The end-point is largely determined by the client's personal goals and ambitions. These may change over time and clients may request help with problems of a different nature.

Intervention: cognitive restructuring

The purpose of this technique is to help clients think more realistically about the situations they perceive to be threatening them; for example to re-evaluate the likelihood that threatening events will occur and what resources they have for dealing with them. Some unrealistic perceptions of threat are quite specific and context dependent. Others arise out of rule-like, dysfunctional assumptions that apply across many situations. Under the heading *cognitive restructuring* I am considering only the more specific and accessible *surface thoughts* associated with distress (see chapter 8 for methods of disputing dysfunctional assumptions). However, as the counsellor begins to uncover the meaning of surface thoughts, it may become evident that they can be related back to a dysfunctional assumption. Disputing these assumptions is likely to be a longer process, for which a client needs greater preparation, so the counsellor should decide early on whether this form of counselling would be helpful to a client and decide, also, whether to offer it.

Preparation for cognitive restructuring
It is essential to explain the role of thought in the elicitation of emotion, using illustrative examples and examples drawn from the client's own account of the problem. This may be supplemented by some suggested reading on the subject (see Appendix A). Some clients claim that they do not have any particular thoughts when they are feeling anxious or experiencing their 'symptoms'. In most cases, a gentle and persistent exploration of the circumstances associated with the problem *does* reveal evidence of irrational thinking.

A client may be well aware that a worry is unrealistic. When viewed dispassionately, the concern about what might happen is not consistent with reality as the client knows it; however, at the height of distress, the belief that something awful will happen seems true, insistent and outweighs any cooler reflection. Clients can be reassured that it will take time and practice for them to think more realistically in distressing situations but that eventually this can be achieved.

It is unlikely that the whole of a session will be given over to cognitive restructuring. The occasion for using it may arise out of a discussion of homework tasks or an incidental remark the client makes during a session. Nevertheless, a counsellor should always announce a move into a restructuring mode so that the client does not feel that at any moment, his/her thoughts will be subjected to critical analysis. The counsellor can say, for example:

'Let's examine the thought you have just expressed.'
'Let's conduct an experiment to see how reasonable this idea is.'
'I want you to examine the evidence you are using for holding this belief.'

Restructuring techniques
There are four main techniques:

– behavioural experiments to test out beliefs;
– examining the meaning of symptoms or feared consequences and

reattributing them to non-threatening (or less threatening) causes;
- disputing irrational thoughts by examining the inferences and evidence used to support them;
- rehearsing actions that, when performed in threatening situations, are likely to lead to a reappraisal of threat.

Behavioural experiments   A client may believe that to do a certain thing is bound to be followed by a catastrophe of some sort. The client is encouraged to test out this belief, on the counsellor's instruction, in order to show that the fear is unfounded. Examples:

A woman who had suffered polio as a child and wore a prosthesis thought that she would fall down, scream and look ridiculous. She was able to travel freely when driving in her car and she could walk away from it within a radius of 100 metres. She was accompanied by the counsellor to a local park and walked to her 'boundary'. At this point, she was asked to fall down and to scream as she did so (the counsellor could have modelled if she had shown reluctance to follow this suggestion). She was then instructed to look around at passers-by and note their reactions. The total lack of interest in her action was a great relief. She immediately felt able to walk a further 50 metres away from her car.

A man was unable to sit opposite another person on a train or bus for fear that he would be stared at. He was concerned that others would notice his discomfort or his blushing. He was instructed to deliberately sit opposite a person and occasionally glance in that direction. His prediction that he would be stared at was disconfirmed and he discovered that others tend to look away when looked at.

A woman feared that she would wet herself if ready access to an exit and/or toilet was denied her. She felt that her bladder was bursting in these situations, even when she had recently emptied it. She agreed to be confined to a locked room for a period of 40 minutes (the counsellor could be alerted by a buzzer if need be). At the end of this period, she was amazed to discover that she had not wet herself, feeling the seat of the chair to confirm the evidence of her own senses. The experiment was repeated after she had drunk a quantity of liquid.

In order to enhance the impact of a behavioural experiment, a client is asked to make before and after estimates of: the likelihood (in percentage terms) of the feared consequences; and the degree of anxiety (on a convenient scale) expected in the situation. Supplementary questions are directed at clarifying the client's explanation of the effect of the experiment. Failed experiments are also valuable in identifying previously unrecognized aspects of a problem. The style of enquiry is not that of 'proving how silly' the client has been. The client identifies the implications through question such as:

> How did the experience compare with what you expected?
> What thoughts were going through your mind when –?
> Why do you think that X did not happen or others did not behave in X way?
> What difference would it make if (the counsellor was not present, the session was longer, X had happened, etc.)?
> Why do you think you were not as frightened on this occasion?
> How does this change your thinking about panic/anxiety occurring in X situation?

The counsellor should summarize the main points learned in the exercise and seek the client's acknowledgement of its accuracy.

Clarifying meaning and reattribution The more a client understands the causes of anxious feelings and attributes them either to realistic existential problems or to harmless natural phenomena, the more a sense of control is achieved. The counsellor uses recent episodes of anxiety, or spontaneous expressions of emotion in the session, to re-educate the client. Diary records should reveal the contribution of entrapment, absence of a safety cue, emotional or physical arousal, natural stressors, caffeine, dreaded events that are not fully acknowledged, and so on.

Reassuring explanations can sometimes be offered for anomalous sensations. The client's perception of the counsellor as knowledgeable about anxiety phenomena sets him or her up as an authority who is trustworthy. A counsellor can capitalize on this by anticipating a 'symptom' he/she thinks the client might have, for example: 'Some people with anxiety problems have strange repetitive thoughts they can't get out of their mind such as doing something disgusting – is that something you have ever experienced?'

Clients frequently ask in a tentative voice whether such-and-such a sensation is 'normal'. They can usually be reassured that the counsellor recognizes this as a sensation that is commonly reported by anxious clients. Where possible, the sensation is attributed not *to* anxiety but to natural processes. Although one should always aim for accuracy, speculative and possibly fictitious explanations are sometimes helpful. The essential point is that the explanation is consistent with the client's use of language and understanding of psychology. For example, Claire Weekes has talked of panic being caused by 'raw nerves' and 'a feeling of being about to collapse' as due to 'muscle weakness'. This style of explanation may suit some clients.

A worry about a missed heartbeat can be countered with the information that the beats are naturally irregular (the more so the lower the average heart rate) and that if the heart speeds up in physical or emotional emergencies, it later compensates by taking a pause in order to revert to its normal rhythm. (Natural explanations of sensations relating to breathing were given earlier in this chapter.) In general, it is helpful to point out that the same sensation experienced in different circumstances is often 'just taken for granted'. A thumping heart is expected after a vigorous run; a person who has just been told that they have inherited a fortune might also feel weak and trembling, and so on.

When a sensation is worrying to a client, the reasons for believing so are explored before an alternative explanation is suggested. Simple reassurance based on the results of medical tests, although necessary, is rarely sufficient because evidence the client is able to produce is not contradicted by the test result. A client who believed that her head was swelling and might explode explained that blood could burst through the walls of vessels in her brain. She gave three sources of evidence for this. First, she experienced a tinnitus whose intensity varied with her pulse. When her pulse rate rose, the tinnitus became unbearably loud. She equated loudness with pressure in her head. The second bit of evidence was derived from the unfortunate result of a medical screening designed to allay her somatic worries. A scan showed evidence of a small, inoperable aneurysm in her head which she was told was 'nothing to worry about'. Lastly, she was being treated by her doctor for high blood pressure.

The fearful thoughts were listed on paper, as below, and the client asked to supply alternative explanations for the sensations (reattribution), and to produce evidence that contradicted her beliefs.

Fearful thoughts:

- I feel that my head is swelling and might explode.
- The blood in my head is under pressure and is going through narrow vessels.

- The blood will burst through the vessel walls.
- Loud sound means that the pressure is building up.
- I have an aneurysm which is a weakness.

The following thoughts to counter her beliefs were listed in an adjacent column.
Alternative explanations and contrary evidence:

- *Feeling* that my head is bigger doesn't mean that it *is* bigger.
- There is no evidence of anyone's head ever bursting open in this way.
- Although I have a slight blood pressure increase, this has been controlled in the past by drugs.
- If the blood supply to the brain was affected I would be more aware of this; in fact my ability to think and reason is normal.
- There is no evidence of my blood vessels being narrow. An aneurysm is a widening not a narrowing of a blood vessel.
- An aneurysm would have burst already with high blood pressure; therefore it is unlikely to burst now.
- If the aneurysm had grown, it would have caused pain or blackouts.
- I have wrongly assumed that when my tinnitus is louder, my blood pressure is higher.

The client was instructed to read over the two sets of thoughts once a day and also when she was bothered by the sensation of her head swelling and bursting. She was also instructed to give up a number of checks she had been carrying out in order to estimate the size of her head. Not only would these checks provide inaccurate feedback but checking also carries the implication that her head *could* swell for the irrational reasons she gave. In learning theory terms, measuring the head is negatively reinforced by a safety signal ('my head is the same size'). Removing this safety cue exposes her to the danger signal ('my head feels swollen') and the opportunity of responding to it differently (for example ignoring the sensation and countering her thoughts with a rational response).

Disputing irrational beliefs   The last example introduced the techniques of disputing irrational beliefs. Cognitive therapists have identified several types of irrational thinking in emotional problems (see Table 7.7) which give rise to specific irrational beliefs. This manual cannot do justice to the full range of cognitive therapy methods, but several examples of the disputing process are

Table 7.7 Types of irrational thinking in anxiety problems

Selective abstraction	The client selects one aspect of a situation and interprets the whole situation on the basis of that one aspect.
Arbitrary inference	The client reaches a conclusion in the face of insufficient evidence or even contrary evidence.
Overgeneralization	From one aspect of a situation the client draws an unwarranted general conclusion.
Magnification and minimization	The client exaggerates negative aspects of a situation and minimizes positive aspects.
Personalization	The client sees external events as reflecting personally on him/herself when there is no basis for making such a connection.

contained within the guided fantasy introduced in chapter 5. The transcript is therefore continued below. It illustrates the processes of disputation and reattribution. Most clients are able to relive anxiety episodes in fantasy, re-experiencing the feelings and thoughts they had at the time. The flexibility of the fantasy technique, and clients' capacity to become immersed in fantasy in a way that mimics reality, make it an eminently suitable vehicle for countering and disputing irrational beliefs. In the following transcript, the logical error associated with an irrational belief is noted alongside the fantasy content. The notes also describe the disputation process.

Continuation of guided fantasy illustrating cognitive restructuring

The client has just recalled an actual incident of being accidentally locked inside someone's flat. A more intense, hypothetical situation of being trapped on a bus is suggested in order to explore her worst fears. (It will be recalled that the client has recently panicked on a bus, and is reliving this experience.)

Transcript	*Notes*
Co: Can you imagine what would happen if you were on a bus and you found you couldn't control the fear. What would happen then?	Present a hypothetical situation to clarify feared consequences.
Cl: I think I'd holler and shout 'Let me out'. And that's very embarrassing.	Lack of control denotes embarrassing consequences for her.
Co: Yes.	Counsellor agrees this is so.

Cl: But I don't think I'd have any control over myself. What can people do – they can't do anything when I think of it in a logical sense.

Co: Try to imagine last night and you can't control the fear. You'd shout out. Try to imagine yourself shouting out.

Suggest the image to increase access to accompanying thoughts.

Cl: Yes. I'd probably cause a riot.

More extreme unpleasant consequence (arbitrary inference and magnification).

Co: A riot?

Cl: You know, people say 'What's wrong'? when the situations arise and there's always some person that causes an upset.

Co: Who would be upset – you or them?

Clarification.

Cl: Me and them, I should think.

Co: What do you think they might do or say?

Request concrete details to elucidate meaning. Clients thinks she would be regarded as mentally ill (arbitrary inference and magnification).

Cl: I'd imagine that they would think I was a bit mental.

Co: Do you sometimes feel that yourself?

Cl: Yes.

Co: What do you understand by 'mental'?

Clarification.

Cl: Well I think there's definitely something wrong mentally. I mean no normal person suffers with this. That's what goes through my mind. When you hear about people who are in wheelchairs and really sick – and they get treatment don't they? And I can't. There's nothing physically wrong with me and I can't even do the simplest things in life.

The evidence she provides is that it is abnormal not to be able to do simple things, there is no physical explanation, no cure, and no excuse for it.

Co:	So you feel ashamed you can't do this?	Interprets client's reasons as likely to induce shame. Further clarification.
Cl:	Yes, that's right.	
Co:	So you're on the bus and let's suppose this has got out of control. You feel you've got to get out. You force your way down the stairs with people looking at you, thinking what's wrong with this woman, she must be mental.	Return to fantasy theme, summarize thought content, and explore further associations.
Cl:	That's right.	
Co:	And you feel embarrassed and ashamed of yourself?	
Cl:	When you look around, there's children on the bus and I think what must they think of a person, an elderly person carrying on like that.	
Co:	Carrying on like a child?	Clarification.
Cl:	Yes, that's right.	
Co:	Do you feel then that you are mentally ill?	Attempt to establish strength of belief. Believes that mental illness causes her fear.
Cl:	I think there's something there that causes it. It's all to do with the mind, isn't it?	
Co:	Do you think there's a difference between being mad and having a strong fear?	Attempt to reattribute cause to 'strong fear'.
Cl:	Well, actually I don't know anyone who is mad. So . . .	Accepts that she has little knowledge to draw the distinction.
Co:	What do you understand by madness?	Clarification.
Cl:	What I hear of anyone that's mad, they also do these same things, don't they – scream and holler.	Concludes that because some mad people shout, she is mad because she feels like shouting when panicky (arbitrary inference).
Co:	Scream and holler?	Clarification.
Cl:	Go hysterical. And those	Her notion of 'mental'

are the thoughts that go through my mind. I'm going to scream and holler.

Co: Do you know anyone who has screamed and hollered like that?

is that of hysteria. She fears losing control of her impulses when panicking.
Examine the evidence that this impulse is associated with being 'mental'.

Cl: No, only what you see on television.

Co: So you have an idea what a mad person is from the television.

Claims no personal knowledge.
Counsellor playing for time while thinking up how to dispute client's arbitrary inferences.

Cl: That's right.

Co: And you imagine yourself acting like that?

Cl: Yes, not in full control of myself.

Co: And you said just now that what happens to you is not logical. [*Pause*]

Counsellor decides to dispute the evidence that a desire to shout is unreasonable when a frightened person is in an enclosed space and that an impulse to shout is natural, not a sign of hysteria.

Cl: That's right. I don't know anyone personally who suffers from this complaint.

Co: What about other fears that people have. Do you know anyone with fears?

Cl: No.

Co: None at all?

Cl: None of my family. My husband's got no fears at all. The only one who has a fear is my neighbour. She's got a fear of the dentist but I suppose a majority of people have got that fear. But I've not got that fear.

Counsellor doubting.
Client argues that other people's fears are normal whereas hers is not.

Co: Do you think that anyone might

Argue that hers is a

Cl: There must be others – otherwise you wouldn't have a name for it.

common fear.

Co: Try to imagine someone locked in a wardrobe. How would most people feel then?

Suggest an extreme example of 'normal' fear.

Cl: I've got no idea.

Client resists this line of argument.

Co: Imagine your husband locked in a wardrobe. You said he doesn't feel fear.

Cl: He has got *no* fear.

Co: So what do you think he would do locked in a wardrobe and unable to open the door?

Cl: I've got no idea.

Co: How do you think he might behave?

Cl: I think he would knock and hope for the best. I think he's that kind of person.

Co: Yes, he might just knock. But some people might holler and shout, mightn't they?

Client probably accepts the point.

Cl: Yes.

Co: What I'm saying is that some people don't like being closed in in small places, do they? This is a normal fear, but you've got it in a more extreme form than most people, haven't you?

Attempt to re-educate and reattribute the impulse to shout.

Cl: Well?

Client not sure.

Co: I think that most people would holler and shout in those circumstances. You might even say that some people would get hysterical but I wouldn't use that word myself. I think it's an extreme fear reaction, not a mental illness.

Cl: Why did I crouch on the floor then?

Client producing evidence for the belief that she has acted hysterically in the past.

Co:	Why did you crouch on the floor?	Pause to think.
Cl:	I'd forgotten all about that till last night.	
Co:	Crouch rather than stand up or sit down?	Clarify meaning.
Cl:	That's right.	
Co:	How did your legs feel? Did you feel that they were weak?	Attempt to use this as evidence of a natural fear response.
Cl:	That's it. The whole of me, I never moved until they knocked the door down.	
Co:	So you felt too weak to stand up?	
Cl:	Yes.	
Co:	So that is why you crouched down then, was it? What you're describing is a very common reaction in extreme fear. People's legs go to jelly. Have you ever heard of that expression before?	The evidence that she crouched is used to reinforce the reattribution to fear.
Cl:	Yes, my legs do go like that when I'm nervous.	
Co:	So what you were experiencing was extreme fear. Your legs going to jelly. Probably your body trembling and crouching was the natural thing to do. What do you think crouching might mean?	Counsellor summarizes and checks out other meanings of crouching for the client.
Cl:	I don't know.	
Co:	Does it seem a strange thing to do?	Pressing for clarification.
Cl:	Yes. I didn't even try to get a screwdriver to take the lock off the door from the inside.	
Co:	So, you found you couldn't think straight, perhaps?	
Cl:	Yes.	
Co:	Well, that is another effect of fear. When you're completely worked up about something you can't concentrate. You can't	Her second piece of evidence is again reattributed to fear, and used to account

| think logically. You can't act rationally because the only thing that is on your mind is your fear and getting away. | for the lack of rationality in her behaviour. |

Although there are advantages, such as spontaneity and immediacy, in countering beliefs during a fantasy, there is less time for the counsellor to marshal his/her thoughts. In other words, it may take some time to analyse what the client is implying, what type of error is being perpetrated, and to think up a strategy for disputing it. An alternative way of proceeding, illustrated earlier, is to take things more slowly in identifying beliefs, writing them down, and giving the client plenty of time to consider the evidence for and against. It is customary to use a sheet drawn up with several columns (see Table 7.8) in which the strength of belief is also rated before and after the countering process. A flow-chart display (see Figure 5.1, p. 65) is also helpful, allowing the client to see more clearly how various components in a vicious cycle operate and how irrational beliefs contribute to it.

The transcript illustrates how the client is drawn into the disputation process through Socratic questioning. The counsellor should check at intervals that he/she has understood the client's meaning, and summarize what has been said. In turn, if the counsellor persuades the client to abstract and interpret the evidence differently, the counsellor should request that the reasoning is repeated back to the counsellor. By requesting likelihood estimates, on a 0–100 per cent scale, at intervals, the decrease in strength of a belief can be charted for the client (for example: how likely is it now that your impulse to shout out is a sign of mental illness?)

Residual doubts and reservations should be listed and disputed, either by means of behavioural experiments or by examining evidence. A useful technique is for the counsellor to take on the beliefs of a client in a reverse role-play; the client then engages in disputing them. The advantage of this technique is that the client has the task of mastering arguments and evidence to dispute their own irrational beliefs role-played by the counsellor. The counsellor can also utilize the additional tactic of playing devil's advocate in order to stretch the client's powers of countering even more extremely expressed beliefs and improbable scenarios.

Table 7.8 *Diary format useful for recording and countering irrational beliefs*

Date	Situation	Emotional distress	Irrational belief(s)	Rational counter	Outcome
	Event, image, memory	1 Describe 2 Rate (0–100)	1 Describe 2 Rate (0–100)	Describe response	Re-rate 1 Emotion 2 Irrat. belief
Mon.	Riding on crowded bus	1 Panic 2 80%	(a) I will scream out (60%) (b) People will think I am mad (80%)	1 I have never done this before 2 Fear is not a mental illness	1 50% (a) 20% (b) 40%

(The example is taken from the guided fantasy, chapter 7, p. 116)

Instruction to client: When you experience an incident of emotional distress, record it in your diary as soon as possible afterwards. Note the date and the situation in which it occurred (including any image or memory that might have triggered it off). Describe the nature of your distress (anxiety, panic, etc.) and rate how severe it was on a scale of 0–100 where 0 is calm and 100 is as distressing as you could imagine that emotion to be. In the next column, write down any irrational thought that went through your mind at the time and rate how strongly you believed it then (0 = not at all; 100 = completely). Attempt to rationally counter the belief by asking the questions about it you have rehearsed in the sessions. Now estimate how strongly you think your emotion would be in the situation and how strongly you believe the irrational thought.

onsolidating progress in cognitive restructuring

The conventional assumption is that if someone is persuaded by an argument on one occasion, the person will adhere to this new position without a further repetition of the reasons for and against. In cognitive restructuring, it is safer to assume that irrational thinking is more like a habit that has to be eroded away rather than wiped away by 'insight'. Moreover, as stated earlier, unless the client is first prepared to accept that an emotion is directly related to the way a situation is *interpreted and thought about*, restructuring is unlikely to be successful.

The cognitive assessment carried out in the first few sessions will not produce a complete picture of the client's irrational beliefs. Common themes should emerge as more and more episodes of anxiety are analysed and discussed. The analysis may suggest behavioural exercises. Through performing them, the client gains valuable feedback information which, at the same time, contributes to the counsellor's cognitive analysis. One can be confident that a process of cognitive change is occurring when a client reports back (sometimes with surprise) that he/she did *not* react to a situation in their habitual manner.

The following techniques help to consolidate cognitive restructuring.

- Encourage the client to identify irrational thoughts and counter them in as many situations as possible.
- To aid recall and rehearsal, ask the client to write down their rational responses to irrational thoughts (e.g. in the ABC diary or in lists) and to read them regularly.
- Within a session, take advantage of any spontaneous comment or emotional reaction that illustrates an irrational thought, and use it as an opportunity for the client to entertain alternative interpretations.
- Use fantasy or role-play to provoke a distressing experience and encourage the client to rehearse rational responses.

Having emphasized that raising the client's awareness of irrational thinking is fundamental, sessions that are devoted to cognitive restructuring should be focused, nevertheless, on just one or two items considered in depth. This avoids overloading and confusing the client, and ensures that the counsellor has covered the full meaning of an irrational thought. As time goes on, cognitive analysis may point to the importance of underlying dysfunctional assumptions. The counselling approach I have outlined above can be developed further to help the client to re-examine the validity of more deeply held convictions (see chapter 8).

Illness fears

As some of the cases discussed earlier have illustrated, a bodily sensation (or 'symptom') can be interpreted by the client as a sign of serious physical illness. A belief in illness becomes irrational when there is no objective evidence to suggest it and all reasonable diagnostic tests have given negative results. Some clients acknowledge that their fear is irrational (i.e. accept that there is no basis for the belief) whereas others really believe that they are physically ill or likely to become so. The strength of this conviction can vary from slight to extreme. The illness may be regarded as an insidious and long-term threat to health, in which case the client does not necessarily expect immediate and catastrophic evidence of the illness during episodes of panic or anxiety.

Illness fear and conviction of illness should not be confused with somatic complaints of, say, pain or nausea for which there is no detectable organic basis. In these clients the primary complaint concerns the symptom (and feeling ill) rather than a fear of what is causing it. It is also important to recognize that many clients have chronic illnesses which, although they are not the primary cause of the anxiety complaint, can contribute to it in subtle ways. For example, respiratory and cardiovascular disorders can contribute to breathing difficulties associated with anxiety. Sensory disabilities such as poor eyesight or hearing loss lower the threshold for fear in certain circumstances. A person with a severe hearing loss cannot hear traffic when crossing a road or the footsteps of a person walking behind them and may develop exaggerated fears of an accident or of being attacked.

A counsellor should routinely ask for a medical history and refer to a physician if any doubt remains about an unexplored physical factor. When a physical disorder is known to be contributing to bodily sensations or discomfort, the client will benefit from help in making clear attributions to physical factors where appropriate and from help in the interpretation of medical advice.

The client may believe in and fear illness on the grounds of the following evidence:

– previous similar illness in self or others close to self (e.g. a friend may have died after a heart attack);
– a family history of some 'weakness' (e.g. heart disease, senility);
– information from the media (e.g. concerning the HIV virus);

- unfamiliar or intense bodily sensations. These may have a real, explicable cause or result from over-attentiveness to the body and represent a heightened awareness of a normal sensation such as the beat of the heart;
- mismanagement of previous illness (in self, family or friends) so that the client lacks faith in medical opinion or treatment. Mismanagement can include a failure to diagnose or a failure to convey the seriousness (or lack of it) of diagnostic findings.

Clients are less likely to exhibit panic attacks associated with illness fears if they do not expect an immediate catastrophic consequence when experiencing the 'symptom' (i.e. the 'illness' has longer-term consequences), and (as noted earlier) if the bodily symptom (assuming there is one) does not escalate in intensity with increased autonomic nervous system arousal mediated by threat. Without these features, the client presents more as being over-concerned and fearful about health. The behavioural consequences of this health anxiety (sometimes referred to as hypochondriasis) are:

- scanning of the body for signs of abnormality leading to a heightened awareness and mislabelling of normal sensations;
- selective attention to illness-related information (in magazines, television programmes, etc);
- excessive checking of parts of the body (e.g. looking in the mirror or feeling parts of the body); ·
- repeated requests for reassurance, especially from members of the medical profession but also from family members. Occasionally a client will make sure that a doctor or hospital is never too far away.

Interventions for illness fears
A client may be reluctant to regard the problem in other than strictly physical terms and this can constitute a serious obstacle to counselling (see chapter 9). Assuming some common ground can be found, the main issue concerns the client's requests for reassurance and tendency to check for ill-health. From the point of view of distinguishing rational from irrational beliefs, it is important to reach agreement on an appraisal of the realistic possibility of becoming ill in the way the client fears. The client may require help in accepting the implications of whatever disorders may actually be present (e.g. raised blood pressure). The appraisal can be made by reviewing the medical evidence for illness (and the client's grounds for disbelieving it) and generating alternative explanations for the

client's 'symptoms'. The counsellor should avoid being drawn into providing reassurance personally and should instead point to the *evidence* that is reassuring. If directly asked for reassurance, the counsellor can say, 'Well, we've looked at the evidence, what conclusion did you come to?' It might be necessary to write to the specialists who have examined the client to obtain first-hand evidence of the findings. Occasionally, but rarely, additional diagnostic screening is required.

It may be possible to generate convincing alternative explanations of specific 'symptoms' (such as stress or over-breathing) especially when diary recording has revealed that they occur in the context of psychologically significant events. One woman, for example, tended to have an attack of vertigo when in the presence of the new wife of her ex-husband.

Certain grounds for a health worry can be disputed by conducting a behavioural experiment. For instance, a client who fears precipitating a heart attack may learn from vigorous exercise that it is quite safe to produce a rapid pulse in this way. A woman who believed that her panics were caused by low blood sugar was encouraged to record systematically her anxiety and blood sugar at prearranged intervals (a testing kit was provided by her doctor). The results convinced her that her explanation was incorrect.

As a general guideline, the client is encouraged to stop all health checks and requests for reassurance. Checks can be cut down gradually if the client is unable to stop them all at once; for example limiting 'routine' visits to the general practitioner to once a month. Situations that are avoided unnecessarily are confronted. A client who avoided eating in salad bars (in case the owner had cut himself and contaminated the food with HIV-infected blood) was encouraged to use them again after appropriate reassurance had been given about the conditions under which the virus can be contracted. By stopping checks and avoidances, a client fully faces up to the source of the health anxiety. The person who provides reassurance might find it difficult to desist. In this case, a verbal or written agreement about the provision of reassurance can be negotiated. The counsellor can act as mediator and explain the rationale to the parties concerned.

In line with earlier guidelines, a brief confrontation with an avoided situation may be insufficient to produce enduring change. The confrontation may have to be repeated and prolonged (for example persistence in reading any magazines regardless of whether they might contain articles on feared illnesses).

Specific traumatic events may have contributed to the origins of an illness fear and the meaning of these events should always be explored: for example blaming self or others for the death of loved ones, anger with certain hospitals or doctors, or anxiety about a life-threatening illness in a person close to the client. In some instances, health anxiety relates to irrational beliefs, which can be restructured as described earlier; for example

> I *must* know exactly why I have this symptom;
> There *must* be a medical solution to my symptoms.

In some cases the health beliefs are better described as dysfunctional assumptions:

> I *ought* to remain completely healthy all my life;
> It is *unfair* that I have to suffer discomfort.

These assumptions can be disputed by methods illustrated in the next chapter.

Suggestions for further reading

Panic attacks have been the subject of great interest recently and a spate of books and articles have been published, covering both theory and practice (e.g. Baker, 1989; Barlow and Cerny, 1988; Clark, 1986; Clark and Beck, 1988; McNally, 1990; Rachman and Maser, 1988; Walker et al., 1991). The role of hyperventilation has been stressed by Ley (1985) and Clark and Salkovskis (1992) in particular. The influence of space and motion stimuli has been considered by Jacob et al. (1989). For illness fears see Warwick and Salkovskis (1990). Useful advice on self-managed confrontation is given in Neuman (1985). The main sourcebook for cognitive therapy of anxiety is Beck et al. (1985). Blackburn and Davidson (1990) also give a clear and practical account.

There are a great many books for the lay person on panic and agoraphobia, but few stand out. Weekes' books are very popular (e.g. Weekes, 1972, 1977) and Neuman (1985), Marks (1980), and Goldstein (1988) can be recommended.

8

Worry, Social Anxiety and Other Pervasive Anxiety Problems

In the problems I am considering now, the client reports being tense, anxious or worried most of the time. The situational triggers for the occurrence of anxiety are less obvious and panic attacks are not the central feature. Avoidance is not prominent and when it is present the reasons behind it tend to be subtle.

Not all clients who are anxious in this general way have the kind of problem I will be describing in this chapter. For instance, an anxiety problem may be pervasive because it has generalized from a specific focus of threat. A person who is afraid of dogs might expect to encounter one whenever they leave home and therefore feel anxious most of the time. Or a client might anxiously expect a panic attack to occur in almost any situation. The way to approach these problems is to work on the specific threat or panic problem from which all else follows.

Pervasive anxiety problems are not yet well understood. I will consider a number of different aspects in turn and simply note that the counsellor is likely to encounter all of these features in different combinations.

Worry about potentially harmful future events

The client's problem is that of persistent and pervasive worrying about potentially harmful or unpleasant events that could happen to anyone but from the client's perspective, seem more likely to happen to him or her, usually with an unrealistically perceived disastrous effect. Worrying may be experienced as compulsive and intrusive. The extent to which the worry is evaluated as realistic varies considerably between clients. Worry about possible negative outcomes of events often interferes with decision-making, leading to doubt and vacillation.

A client might say that he/she has always been a 'worrier' or a 'nervous person' and does not really expect to change in this respect. These clients tend to seek help when life has become unduly stressful and their habit of worrying has got out of hand. Almost any aspect of life can form the focus of worry (e.g. family, finances, work, health) and one aspect may become prominent because a specific stress has arisen, such as moving home. Clients whose prevailing mood is depressed are also likely to express worries in one or more of these areas. Population surveys have shown that generalized worrying is the most common form of anxiety problem but it seems that people who experience life in this way are less likely to seek counselling assistance than those who have panic attacks or specific fears. The latter restrict a person's life in more obvious ways.

Intervention: stimulus control

The aim is to minimize the number of occasions on which worry is likely to occur and to maximize the number of pleasant, relaxing, worry-free periods. The assumption is made that certain environmental situations trigger off worrying, or conversely, pleasant thoughts. Diary recording may have revealed what these are. The client can be asked: 'What activities help you to forget your worries?' or 'In what situations do you worry less?'

One client, an accountant, worked from home, and the sight of his papers tended to provoke worrying thoughts. He was encouraged to segregate work and leisure activities, by both time and place: to confine work to one office environment, to have a separate work telephone, to switch on an answering-machine when 'off-duty' and to receive clients within appointed hours only. The client was instructed to arrange non-work areas so as to facilitate leisure activities (reading, listening to music, etc.).

The sorts of activity that best promote *non-worrying* are those that require intense visual involvement and motor coordination, such as craftwork, mechanical tasks, sports and painting. These activities are likely to engage the client's attention fully, providing distraction from worrying thoughts. Clients can sometimes gain greater respite from worrying by taking a walk in a pleasant environment than by engaging in relaxation training. Clients should be encouraged to rearrange their activities in a systematic way and to record them so that they can be monitored by the counsellor.

Another strategy which may help is that of instructing the client to indulge in worrying only at certain times of the day (e.g. a 30-minute period in the early evening). The instructions to the client in this technique are as follows:

- Become aware of your worrying and identify when worrying starts as early as possible in the sequence.
- As soon as you catch yourself worrying, postpone the worry until your 'worry period'.
- Instead of worrying give your full attention to what you are doing and the immediate surroundings.
- Set your 30-minute worry period for the same time and same place each day.
- During your worry period, worry intensely about whatever you were concerned about earlier, for the whole half-hour period.

Indecision, vacillation and ineffectual problem-solving

The association between worry and indecision was noted earlier. In many cases worry relates to future improbable events over which the worrier has no direct influence: for example a client may worry when a family member takes a flight. However, clients also worry about day-to-day decisions and realistic stressors but the action taken (if any) is often ineffectual. The source of worry can be presented to the client as a problem that can be solved rationally. This approach is normally readily understood because it is rare that a client lacks the ability to solve problems effectively in all areas of his/her life. Problem-solving involves the following steps:

- The parameters of the problem must be defined so that the client is able to state what outcome he/she prefers, what outcome must, at all costs, be avoided, what is a tolerable fallback position ('the bottom line') and what constraints there are over the client's course of action.
- A list of possible actions and their consequences is generated, together with the advantages and disadvantages of each one.
- A means of weighing the advantages and disadvantages is followed and a decision is made.
- The client reports back on the actual consequences of the decision and reflects on the original formulation of the problem in light of the outcome.

The stressful events about which the client worries are identified through diary recording. When the stress is short term and the outcome is reported back, the counsellor invites the client to discuss the relative merits of the chosen solution and other options and to reflect on what has been learned from the actual outcome.

Attempts to formulate the problem may bring to light irrational beliefs which can be countered or disputed as described in chapter 7.

The inability to produce an effective solution to a problem is occasionally attributable to a lack of skill or knowledge, for example how to produce an assertive response, in which case skills training may be the preferred intervention.

The following client illustrates how a problem-solving discussion of what, for her, was a worrying decision led to the identification of irrational beliefs. These distorted her evaluation of the evidence she was using to make her decision and contributed to the emotional distress she experienced.

The client worried excessively over a decision she had to make between travelling some considerable distance to attend the wedding of a friend or to stay at home and spend the time with a man to whom she was very attracted, but had met only recently. She was very pleased to receive the wedding invitation but could barely afford to travel so far. The advantages and disadvantages of attending and not attending were listed. Not to attend signified not only loss of enjoyment but also loss of an occasion on which she would be validated as a person esteemed by her friend. She felt that not attending would also send a signal to her male friend that she was not an independent person and that, in fact, she was remaining at home in order to be with him; she would then think less of herself for not being more independent.

The decision had presented itself as a straightforward profit and loss choice between attractive alternatives but this did not account for her persistent worrying and concern about making the right decision. In fact, the systematic examination of alternatives indicated that the crucial pay-offs concerned her self-esteem. Lacking confidence that others really approved of her for her own qualities, she attempted to ensure their approval by doing what she imagined would please them most. However, recognizing this tendency in herself, she also wanted to give the impression that she was independent of others' approval.

Formulating the alternatives in this way she recognized:

- that neither accepting the invitation nor giving up the opportunity to consolidate her relationship at home would substantially affect how these significant friends valued her;
- that if she wished to feel valued by them, she could achieve this in other ways, e.g. by making sure that if she refused the invitation an opportunity was created for another meeting in the medium-term future;
- that she could increase her self-esteem by paying off financial debts to friends rather than spend the money on travel.

Recognizing her dependence on feeling valued by others, she was anxious not to give the impression of being 'clingy'. However, she was unclear about what would count as 'clinging' and what would count as a perfectly ordinary expression of her needs. She was helped to formulate criteria and was then able to see that:

– not to accept the invitation would not imply that she was clinging to her new male acquaintance;
– she could act in such a way as to create any desired impression
  of the reasons for remaining at home.

An important element of the problem-solving approach is to encourage clients to take control of events rather than see themselves as the victim of circumstances. This particular woman reported back later on the consequences of her decision not to attend the wedding and how this resolution had enhanced rather than diminished her self-esteem.

Counselling had identified a dysfunctional assumption ('I need everyone to value me and I must not give up any opportunity to gain the approval of others'). Holding this assumption, a large number of situations were perceived as reflecting on her self-worth. In cases such as this, episodes of distress recorded in a diary are likely to reflect repeatedly the same themes. The dysfunctional assumption can be countered *proactively* by techniques described below.

Dysfunctional assumptions

This section carries forward principles and techniques introduced in earlier chapters. The initial stage of counselling is often taken up with the alleviation of the most urgent complaints of the client, leaving little opportunity for identifying and countering dysfunctional assumptions. The following guidelines are addressed to these tasks.

The belief held by the woman described above, that she should always seek the approval of others, illustrates the chief features of dysfunctional assumptions. Her example also shows, incidentally, how an awareness of a major concern or vulnerability can lead a client to overcompensate. For example, this woman set out to project an image of independence for the benefit of the man to whom she was attracted. These attempts to compensate may back-fire and perpetuate the misconceived assumption. For instance, if correctly intuited by another, they may cause the other to act as if the person *is* dependent, thereby confirming that person's own self-opinion.

A dysfunctional assumption has the following characteristics:

- It is a *broad* assumption influencing perception of self and others in many situations.
- It operates in an automatic, habitual way so that its detection and modification requires effort.
- It might be held with deep conviction.
- It can be conceptualized in an abstract, rule-like form.

The feature that makes the assumption dysfunctional, when considered rationally, is that it is held in a rigid, absolute form. The person responds inflexibly to certain types of situation. It is therefore vital that the counsellor works sensitively in helping the client to become aware of the assumptions he or she appears to be making. Moreover, it is quite likely that the dysfunctional assumption has arisen in the context of early family experiences or trauma in which context the assumption may have been part of an adaptive response to a difficult situation. The client may wish to avoid discussion of these memories. If so, the client is encouraged to open up or, at the least, make meaningful connections between present and past circumstances. This may enable the client to see that assumptions valid in the past are no longer so in the present.

When clarifying a client's beliefs, the counsellor should avoid the tendency which is hard to resist, of supplying an analysis *for* the client. Clients benefit more from articulating, however inadequately, their own thoughts than from receiving a clever summary from the counsellor. Holding back in this way is a difficult skill to acquire and there is a danger of falling into lecturing, preaching, or even bombarding the client with counter-arguments. This form of persuasive pressure is clearly unhelpful.

The following guidelines are offered to help the counsellor counteract these tendencies:

- Introduce the client to basic concepts of cognitive therapy (by using examples from the client's life, or life in general) of the direct relationship between the interpretation of a situation and the emotion experienced. Books written for the lay person can be useful in this educational phase (see Appendix A).
- Use a Socratic style of questioning, allowing the client to draw out the implications of what has been said (e.g. what inferences have been made, how different statements reflect a common theme or a contradiction). Some useful questions are:

'What is your evidence for believing that?'

'What alternative explanations might there be?'

'How might someone else (your peers, partner, colleagues) view that?'

'Please explain your reasoning there.'

'Can you see any contradiction in the way you have phrased that?'

'Do you think you might be overlooking any contrary evidence?'

'You have stated that as a black and white alternative – do you think there is any middle ground?'

'Try to tell me what your underlying belief might be in the situation you have just described.'

- Don't answer the question for the client. Gently extract the information.
- Have a clear purpose in asking a question (avoid rapid-fire questions without a clear conceptualization of what it is you are clarifying).
- Ask specific, direct questions.
- Time the question to facilitate rapport, i.e. don't return to a topic which has been adequately discussed or break into a client's chain of thinking by introducing a different topic. As a general rule, deal with issues that are uppermost in the client's mind in that session. Question the client's priorities rather than ignoring them.
- Explore only one or two themes in depth in a session rather than moving rapidly from one set of ideas to another.
- Allow time (for yourself and the client) to ponder the meaning of what is said. Ask, for example, 'Can you think of anything else that might relate to this?'
- Use the client's terminology where possible, e.g. one client was upset by the contradictory messages he was getting from his work supervisor and he saw the implications of this in catastrophic terms. He felt he was not being allowed 'a level playing field'. It was remarked that he was seeing the playing field as 'tipped vertical' rather than just tilting a little. In this way, the idea of black and white thinking was conveyed in a form that was easy for him to assimilate.

Intervention: modifying dysfunctional assumptions

The aim is to help clients see that they are evaluating events against standards that are too rigid and over-generalized when looked at rationally after considering the evidence. A client might believe that things *ought or must* be viewed in a certain way because otherwise (and this is usually unstated by the client) things would be out of control or catastrophic. Some techniques for identifying dysfunctional assumptions are:

– finding a common assumption in several examples. The client is invited to consider a number of statements expressing his/her thoughts or beliefs and to find a general assumption to link them. If the client is unable to do this, the counsellor puts forward several suggestions for linking the examples, and invites the client to discuss their merits. If a suggestion is agreed, it should be rephrased in the client's own words (e.g. 'What, then, is the best way to sum up the linking idea? Please put it in your own words.')

– extracting the hidden complement to the overt statement of belief or evaluation. I can illustrate this by returning to the woman mentioned above. In response to her remark 'I hate to refuse an invitation', she was asked 'Why is it bad to refuse an invitation occasionally?' Her reply indicated that invitations counted as evidence that people valued her and, further, that refusing would mean both that people would value her less and that she needed (*had* to have) these validations of her worth.

– the downward arrow technique in which each response of the client is responded to with 'And what would that mean to you?' or 'What would be so bad about that?' (This was described in chapter 4.)

The aim of the intervention is to help the client identify an assumption and weaken the rigidity of its application. It is neither feasible nor desirable to have the aim of modifying radically a client's core assumptions about self and world. Much can be achieved with the gentle Socratic style of questioning alone. As clients begin to articulate the meaning of their statements, they are often struck by the way they have stated them in an extreme or absolute manner.

The following additional techniques may be helpful:

– Questioning the utility of the assumption, e.g. leading the client to acknowledge that holding the assumption leads to considerable suffering. How does it help to achieve other objectives the client holds? Asking the client to make a list of the advantages and disadvantages of an assumption can help to bring home the costs of holding an assumption in a rigid, absolute form. The exercise may lead the client to adopt a less extreme version of the assumption.

– Highlighting the *context* in which an assumption was learned (e.g. the social or cultural context or unreasonable parental demands). This may help the client to understand that what was *once* useful is no longer so. In the new context (and with adult resources) the assumption can be reviewed and re-evaluated.

– Disputing the evidence for an assumption. The application of this technique to specific beliefs was described earlier. The purpose in disputing the evidence is to show that it does *not* in fact support the truth of the dysfunctional assumption. This may be demonstrated by disputing the logic of an inference, by showing that the evidence is open to alternative interpretations, or by pointing out inconsistencies in the way the client has utilized the evidence.

– Showing that the assumption itself is invalid. For example, the client may believe that 'If I do everything competently, I will be rewarded.' The client is invited to consider personal instances, or examples from life in general, where the assumption does not hold.

– Reality testing. The suggestion is made that a client act in such a way as to violate a personal assumption in order to verify its consequences. For example, a client is asked to refuse a request from a friend in order to test out whether he/she will be rejected. A client who believes that it is always wrong to be selfish is given the homework assignment of acting selfishly. A discussion of the consequences of these exercises is likely to lead to a reformulation of the assumption in a more flexible form.

An inability to relax

A client may report difficulty in relaxing mentally, physically, or both. Mental over-arousal is indicated by frequent intrusive thoughts; these may take the form of worries, mental checks, or simply a rehearsal of relatively meaningless thoughts such as the contents of a shopping list. Clients who are hypervigilant for threat are likely to be distracted by bodily or other cues, thereby preventing a descent into the less focused, pleasant reverie associated with relaxation.

A constant preparation for threat is likely to leave the client muscularly tense, fatigued and with a sympathetic predominance in the activity of the autonomic nervous system. Breathing and pulse may quicken and become irregular, digestion is inhibited, and cold sweats are common. Muscular tension may be expressed as headache or other pain, as foot-tapping, pacing or muscle twitches.

What I have just described is regarded by many as the 'essence' of anxiety and they advocate its 'management' through the application of 'coping skills' such as a quick relaxation response. The philosophy I want to convey in this book is that anxiety problems should be addressed at source after careful analysis. When this has been done, there is often no need to implement further techniques for controlling 'anxiety' as such. However, for selected clients (and it is difficult to state what distinguishes them), learning to relax can be invaluable. In fact, the mental ease that comes with deep relaxation may be experienced as novel and refreshing.

Before employing any training technique, it is worth checking that the client's lifestyle is conducive to relaxation:

1 Check intake of tea, coffee, or other stimulants/medications and advise a reduction where appropriate.
2 Check the balance of work and rest activities, and sleep pattern. Help the client to identify and expand relaxing activities. Use psychological strategies to manage a sleep problem.
3 Check that the client is exercising regularly.

Intervention: relaxation (lifestyle approach)
To a large degree, relaxation is a matter of lifestyle and personal philosophy. To do things in a relaxed fashion and to accept the unavoidable upsets of life is to take a certain attitude towards the world. This approach to relaxation can be contrasted with learning a relaxation response as a skill to regulate anxious arousal in specific situations. The coping skill approach may be of value to clients who otherwise have the capacity to relax in a general sense.

For clients who generally find it difficult to 'switch off' mentally or physically, a relaxation training programme can be a useful component in a broader strategy of lifestyle change. An experience of relaxing deeply in the counsellor's office can spur a client on to take the process much further through their own efforts. However, the beneficial effects of training may not be noticeable for two or three months and the client should be made aware of this fact.

Relaxation training has three main objectives, which are to teach the client:

- to differentiate states of arousal/tension from a state of relaxation;
- to detect the early signs of becoming tense and to change behaviour before a spiral of arousal/tension has developed;
- to acquire techniques for facilitating relaxation and to learn to conduct daily activities with a lesser, but appropriate, degree of effort.

The client is given the rationale, first, that it is possible to develop the ability to relax through regular practice and, second, that this ability will make it easier to conduct all activities in a more relaxed style. For example, sitting, standing, walking, driving and eating can all be approached differently. The components of training are:

– Teach the client to relax deeply in the counsellor's office (usually requiring 2–5 sessions).
– Instruct the client to practise at home once or twice a day for 20–30 minutes, initially using audiotaped instructions, and later without. Any difficulties in doing this are reported back to the counsellor.
– The client is instructed to self-observe when carrying out various activities and to deliberately relax if tense (e.g. adjust body posture, relax tense muscles, exhale and drop shoulders). A system for prompting self-observation can be helpful (e.g. an event that occurs at intervals during the day). Systematic diary recording of periods of tension may provide a client with the necessary information to anticipate tension and to relax at its earliest signs.

A variety of methods of learning to relax more deeply have been described in the literature and there appears to be little research evidence to indicate that one is superior to another. I have evolved a combination of methods, described below. (Readers who want to adopt a purist approach are referred to the suggested reading.) The office-based session can be audiotaped for the client (or recorded separately in quieter conditions) or a commercial tape obtained. It is essential for home practice that the client is able to reserve an uninterrupted quiet period during the day in a warm room. A firm bed, thick carpet, or comfortable chair with headrest is recommended.

Procedure for relaxation training Office environment: this should be reasonably quiet, telephone disconnected, bright lights dimmed, fitted with couch or comfortable chair with headrest. Instruction to client: to attend to the counsellor's voice and follow his/her suggestions. The aim is to facilitate relaxation, a normal state, not to hypnotize the client. The client is asked to report on any difficulties he/she encounters. The client is asked to loosen tight clothing and close the eyes.

Suggestions to the client: these are given in a relaxed, soothing voice. They combine the following elements which can be ordered as suggested below.

1. Focus on actual bodily sensations in a particular part of the body, working from toes to head; e.g. 'Feel the sensations that are coming from your feet and ankles. If you feel any tension, focus on the tension, feel the tension, and gradually it will begin to fade and disappear.' (Note that groups of muscles are not first tensed

up as in some techniques. The only advantage I have observed in doing this is that the feeling of tension may become more obvious by slightly tensing up already tense muscles. Any client who has joint or muscle problems should not be asked to tense up.)

2. Suggest warmth, heaviness, limpness and relaxation in the whole body or particular parts; e.g. 'Feel the sensations of warmth and heaviness spread through your feet and ankles'; 'You may feel your feet tingle a little as they become more and more relaxed.'

3. Breathing pattern: Encourage diaphragmatic rather than thoracic breathing, and also natural, unforced breathing; e.g. 'Now become aware of your breathing. Just breathe normally and gently. Become aware of your stomach rising as you breathe in and falling as you breathe out. As you breathe out, make sure you expel all the air. As you do so feel your chest relax and your shoulders drop down. As you breathe out, feel a wave of relaxation spread down your arms and down your body. Pause for a moment after breathing out and enjoy the sensation. Don't worry about breathing in, that will take care of itself. (Note the emphasis on normal breathing and its automatic nature. I have observed that deliberate attempts to manipulate breathing, apart from pausing between breaths and encouraging diaphragmatic breathing, can be counter-productive. However, systematic breathing retraining can be helpful in clients who hyperventilate; see chapter 7.)

4. Mental relaxation: The client conjures up an image of a favourite (relaxing) place or the counsellor suggests a prepared scene such as a beach or country scene. The client is asked to focus on the concrete imagery of the scene (touch, smell, lights, sounds), details of which may be suggested. The client is told that if irrelevant thoughts come to mind, he/she is to return to the scene and elaborate upon it. The scene serves to occupy the mind with relaxing imagery and provides a means of diverting attention from negative, intrusive thoughts. Suggestions for deepening relaxation can be included in the scene: e.g. 'Imagine some steps going down to the beach. You are at the top of the steps. With each step you take, allow yourself to become more and more relaxed, more and more at peace with yourself', etc.

Order of combination of the elements This is a matter of choice, although I have found the following sequence effective:

1 whole body focus ('Feel your body sinking down, feel the points of contact with the chair', etc.);
2 part body focus; first feet, toes, ankles, then lower and upper legs, buttocks;

3 breathing pattern attended to as above, body focus on chest, shoulders, then arms and hands;
4 body focus on head and neck (forehead, cheeks, jaw, tongue and eye muscles);
5 elaboration of mental imagery (10–15 minutes);
6 return to steps 1–4;
7 say: 'In a few minutes, I will count down from five to one. When I reach one, open your eyes and gradually arouse yourself';
8 seek feedback from the client on areas of residual tension, ability to adopt diaphragmatic breathing, effectiveness of imagery or any other problems.

A client may feel embarrassed in the first one or two sessions and if this becomes evident the reasons should be explored. Distress may be caused by a fear of losing control. In some cases, the client is upset by thoughts that surface in the relaxed state. It is rare that any of these obstacles are long-lasting if sensitively handled. The exercise can be continued in modified form if necessary (e.g. with eyes open).

Applied relaxation
The aim of applied relaxation training is to teach the client to employ a rapid relaxation response (RRR) to diminish their fearful reaction to specific situations. The procedure is viewed as the equivalent of acquiring a new coping response. This is not the only application of relaxation, of course. Interventions involving imagery and covert rehearsal of behaviour (or 'mental practice') are usually carried out more successfully when the client is first relaxed. The following is a brief description of the steps in the applied relaxation technique (for more detail, see 'Suggested reading').

Explain the rationale as follows: 'Learning to relax is a skill that can be acquired with practice and you can use it to reduce your anxiety reactions to events that occur in your daily life. In addition to teaching you the RRR, I will ask you to keep a diary record of the times that you feel tense or anxious. This will enable you to learn to recognize which kinds of situation trigger these reactions in you. The aim is also to help you to learn the bodily sensations that give warning of a build-up of tension. As you begin to learn to recognize them, you will be able to use your RRR to bring the tension under control before it becomes intense. But first I will teach the RRR and show you how you can associate it with a particular word like "relax" or "calm". Saying the word to yourself will help you to relax more quickly.'

The client is taught deep relaxation, gradually fading out the verbal prompts from the counsellor or from audiotaped instruction. The client is taught a rapid body-focusing method (e.g. toes to head) in order to reduce the amount of time to relax to a few minutes only.

The counsellor teaches the client to associate a sub-vocal word (one the client prefers, such as 'relax' or 'peace') with each exhalation together with suggestions from the counsellor to relax deeply. The time taken to relax is reduced in this phase to about 20–30 seconds.

The client practises using the RRR to reduce his/her response to brief (10–15 seconds) anxiety-inducing images suggested by the counsellor. The client may find it helpful to take a deep breath before exhaling and saying the cue word. The body is scanned so that areas of tension can be released. This skill is extensively practised until it is effective in reducing anxiety or tension rapidly in the office situation. In addition to imagery, relaxation can be practised to counter stressful *in vivo* exercises, e.g. a mock interview.

The client practises using the RRR in the home and everyday environment, having been alerted to triggering situations in the self-monitoring phase. The aim is to employ it as early as possible before tension/anxiety escalates. Use of the technique and its effectiveness are recorded in the diary and monitored in this way by the counsellor.

Case illustration: a man who worries excessively and is over-aroused

Mr. R. is a 57-year-old lecturer who is presently on sick leave. He has a chronic medical ailment which does not prevent him from working but it adds to the stress he experiences at work. He reports being anxious and irritable in many situations and is inclined to lose his temper when aggravated by students who are 'disrespectful, even insolent'. He feels 'trapped' when driving in traffic and hates queuing in shops. He 'cannot relax' and has difficulty getting off to sleep. He suffers from headache and tiredness, and describes himself as 'on the verge of a nervous breakdown'. He worries constantly about work and family matters, especially the safety of family members when travelling. He checks at night that gas taps are turned off and doors are locked. He fears that he will 'break down' if things continue as they are. At first interview he appears restless and agitated and talks without pausing.

Outline of the problem   External factors: He has always enjoyed his work but organizational changes and additional responsibility in recent years have placed increasing demands upon him. He has felt the need to work longer hours, including some weekends, and he has not taken his full holiday entitlement. He has decided to apply for early retirement and is currently faced with the uncertainty of whether it will be granted and how he will cope if it is not. His medical condition can be regarded as an external factor and something he could not have foreseen. He reports no other external stressors and he lives in a comfortable home with a loving and supportive family.

Internal factors: He identifies his 'perfectionism' and 'tendency to worry' as primarily responsible for his predicament. Recently, 'getting things done to my high standards' has become increasingly laborious. Work has become stressful and he has not managed to reduce the demands he places on himself. This is not through lack of problem-solving ability. He lists upcoming tasks and, without prompting, has itemized the advantages and disadvantages of four different options for resolving his work stress. He has been able to choose one of them (early retirement) and act on his decision. However, his method of problem-solving is as follows. Lists are meticulously typed into a word processor. He has devised an extensive data base for his correspondence, bills, and some other relatively minor matters. Part of his evening is taken up with an updating of this information.

Mr R.'s aims: he has a clear idea of the factors that have led up to his current difficulties. His main aim is to 'give up work and adopt a sensible lifestyle'. He wants to 'slow down and switch off'. He considers that his high standards have generally been a help rather than a hindrance in his career up to this point and he prefers to reduce his commitments rather than compromise his standards.

Formulation: Mr R. has already chosen his path of escape from work stress but as long as he remains uncertain whether his request for early retirement will be accepted, he is likely to continue to worry about his situation. This places limits on what can be expected of methods that aim directly at helping him to 'slow down and relax'. Yet he seems willing to modify his lifestyle if not his standards of performance. We can speculate that he holds a rigid assumption of the type 'I *must* do things perfectly'. However, he might be willing to be more flexible in this respect. For example, part of his self-imposed workload seems to have been generated by attempts to deal with relatively trivial matters in too thorough a way. Assuming that he is motivated to avoid the aversive consequences of doing things to lower standards, it is important to find out what these consequences are, how severe they appear to be to him, and how closely they match the actual consequences of a lowering of standards.

Initial aims and interventions:

1 to support Mr R. and offer advice if requested until his retirement plans have been confirmed;
2 to encourage Mr R. to reduce activities motivated by perfectionist standards and to gently dispute his assumption that he *must* do things perfectly;
3 to cognitively restructure situations about which Mr R. worries on a daily basis (e.g. family obligations, health and safety);
4 to facilitate relaxing and enjoyable activities.

Mr R. was seen at intervals of 2–4 weeks for nine months.

Outcome:

1.   Support – Mr R. was granted his request after seven months and made good use of the support and advice he was offered over this period. He was predictably relieved by the outcome.

2.   Perfectionism – the origins of his perfectionism and why it was important to him were discussed. He concluded that work and domestic chores would not be enjoyable unless done to his high standards. However, he agreed that it would be advisable to limit the number of tasks he undertook and to revise his standards for 'low-priority' tasks. Mr R. was able to refuse requests from his college 'to help out'. He prioritized his daily list of tasks into high, medium and low priority and was able to dispense with the last of these in most cases.

3.   Daily worries – he was able to re-evaluate his inflated estimates of the probability of unpleasant events befalling him or his family. (Enquiry revealed a history of a traumatic event that had sensitized him to the possibility of family accidents.)

4.   Relaxation – Mr R. was highly aroused both mentally and physically. Simply sitting with me for an hour without pacing or ruminating on his worries was an achievement in itself. Relaxation exercises were carried out with partial success in the office but he was unable to practise relaxation at home. More was achieved by instructing him to work more slowly on tasks, not to set himself stringent deadlines, and to build in regular walks in places of interest to him. He was instructed to walk more slowly with a relaxed posture and to be especially observant of things around him. Under such conditions Mr R. was able occasionally to 'relax and forget himself'.

Pervasive social anxiety

'Social anxiety' is a blanket term that refers to problems ranging from discomfort in quite circumscribed situations (such as giving a speech) to distress that pervades almost all social interactions. Circumscribed social anxieties usually respond to techniques described in earlier chapters. Pervasive anxiety problems are more complex and in this section I offer some conceptualizations that may help in assessment. The approach I advocate is intended to influence the client primarily through the medium of homework assignments and discussion of actual incidents in the client's life. In comparison with other anxiety problems, pervasive social anxiety is more intricately interwoven into the client's life circumstances and these can be changed only gradually. For example, developing a network of friends, forming new intimate relationships or changing an occupation are likely to take months or years rather than weeks. Critical 'distressing events' may occur infrequently so that the length of counselling may have to be extended to allow time for the client to test out and consolidate new ideas and new behaviours.

Counselling is itself a social interaction and a client may feel threatened by exposing what is perceived to be 'inadequacy' and consequently feel reluctant to be counselled. It is therefore important to establish a solid basis of trust before intervening. The content of the interaction between client and counsellor during the session can sometimes be used as a basis for discussion and cognitive restructuring. In my view this should not be the primary purpose of the counselling relationship; the method I advocate relies on influencing social interactions in the client's own milieu.

The assessment should take seriously the possibility that a client's problems are an understandable consequence of external circumstances, even though the client may be inclined to pathologize them or see him/herself as to blame. For example, a highly anxious gay man felt that he had to put on a false front at work, such as laughing at jokes directed at gays. Although he could not countenance being open about his sexual orientation in his present occupation, he came to realize that he would be far less anxious in an environment in which his sexual orientation was not an issue. As a result, he planned significant changes in his lifestyle and mode of employment. Another client was a 40-year-old single woman, most of whose friends were married. She avoided many social situations and especially large parties. In the course of clarifying her goals, she realized that she was unlikely ever to enjoy the sort of parties she had been attending and that she had outgrown many of her old friends. A lifestyle change in which she took more initiative in directing her social life gave her more social satisfaction with less anxiety.

Conceptualizations of social anxiety

Many clients do not overtly avoid social situations because this would be too costly; they prefer to maintain their work and leisure activities as far as possible. Nevertheless, more subtle forms of avoidance such as minimal participation and 'glazing over' are common. Many clients use alcohol to get themselves through their social encounters and with this assistance they may enjoy them. It is evident, then, that many socially anxious people persistently confront social situations but do not benefit by feeling less anxious. This demands an explanation given the importance I have attached to confronting the anxiety-eliciting situation. The following hypotheses (which are not mutually exclusive) have been put forward to account for the lack of spontaneous lessening of distress. The general argument is that social interaction is extremely complex and a person will not spontaneously become less distressed unless they are capable of analysing their difficulty and are willing to change the standards by which they judge their own performance and that of others.

Lack of social skill A person who has not acquired the skills needed to read social situations accurately or to reciprocate the approach of another is unlikely to be socially successful. The individual will report anxiety if, in addition, he/she is aware of the lack of skill and perceives that others are evaluating an interaction negatively. When there is a fear of criticism or rejection, a client may be inhibited from exercising skills that are well within his/her capacity to employ. Anxiety problems in which a lack of skill is prominent may respond to rehearsal of assertiveness and other social skills in role-play or real-life situations. It is beyond the scope of this manual to include guidelines on skills training but fortunately there are many excellent books to which the reader may turn (see suggestions for further reading.)

Interference with social performance   The presence of a high degree of bodily arousal and worrying thoughts about social performance are liable to interfere with the smooth execution of a social interaction. Thus, a person who becomes aware of being observed, or notices that their heart is thumping or that they are blushing or trembling, is likely to focus attention on their thoughts and sensations rather than on the social encounter itself. The person is distracted and cannot fully attend to relevant social cues; consequently the cues are not available to be utilized. In extreme cases, the person's mind 'goes blank'. This in turn can lead to a negative response from another person. In many cases, however, a client overestimates the extent to which their performance falls short of (what they imagine to be) the expectations of other people.

A person is especially prone to become self-focused when the signs of bodily arousal are visible (e.g. trembling, blushing, twitching). These reactions may distress the client even though they are barely noticed by another person or, if noticed, receive no adverse comment. It is when a person feels least confident or under scrutiny that self-focus is most likely to have a deleterious effect on performance.

Causal misattribution   It has been observed that socially anxious people tend to blame themselves for unsuccessful social encounters when an alternative interpretation for failure would be equally plausible. Conversely, they are reluctant to take the credit when things go well, preferring to attribute success to luck or special circumstances. These persistent biases mean that they do not obtain accurate feedback and are slow to learn how to modify their own social performances. One explanation for these causal attributions is that a person believes that they should please others and that others will be less displeased if they take the blame for failure. A high degree of self-criticism is also a strategy for preventing oneself from repeating the same blunders. Moreover, a strategy of *not* taking credit has the advantage that others will not expect the person to maintain an equally good performance in future.

Maladaptive beliefs   The concept of rationality is not as easily applied to the social world as it is to the perception of physical dangers. Yet even if we cannot clearly regard a person's beliefs about self or others as irrational, the beliefs may not be widely shared and may lead to a persistent misinterpretation of social situations and a negative reaction from others. In this sense the beliefs are maladaptive and a client may fairly readily admit that this is the case. Social anxiety can sometimes be traced to the effects of maladaptive and inflexibly held beliefs of the following kind:

- A client over- or underestimates his/her capacities or attributes.
- A client believes that the standards by which they judge their own performance should be rigidly adhered to under all circumstances.

– A client wrongly believes that they are being judged and evaluated by others in a certain way.

For example, people who expect to be criticized by others (because they don't meet the standards they set themselves or the standards they believe others to judge them by) are likely to interpret ambiguous, or even neutral, social feedback as reflecting on their performance or global self-worth. Another's silence may be interpreted as 'being ignored' or 'being passed over' whereas in fact this is a misreading of the other person's intentions. It is also likely that a person's expectation of being ignored will influence his/her behaviour in advance, so that the expectation of being ignored becomes self-fulfilling. Thus, non-verbal cues such as looking away, which reflect the person's ambivalence about interacting, may signal to the other person a lack of positive interest in engaging in a social encounter.

Chronically low self-esteem   A person's social anxiety may relate to a perception of self as an unworthy, insignificant individual, which is an example of a dysfunctional assumption discussed earlier in this chapter. These self-perceptions often relate back to damaging, abusive or traumatic past experiences. It may prove necessary for the client to learn to recognize the assumptions that he/she is making and to retrieve and restructure these memories of damaging relationships. This topic takes us outside the scope of this manual.

Interventions for pervasive social anxiety

Self-managed confrontation and skill rehearsal based on diary recording   It is only rarely that the general aim of confronting anxiety-provoking situations can be fulfilled by contrived simulations. Counselling in groups has obvious advantages in providing a social matrix, and the popularity of assertiveness training courses suggests that standard exercises are helpful. In this section I will limit myself to describing an individual approach which focuses on the client's daily activities. It aims to work indirectly through homework assignments. Incidents are recorded in the client's anxiety diary and are analysed retrospectively; anticipated situations are prepared for prospectively. This approach ensures that the problems discussed in counselling are salient, relevant, and that their resolution is likely to have immediate consequences for the client. In summary, client and counsellor work as follows:

1 The client reports back on recent incidents of social interaction or homework assignments.

2 Difficulties are pinpointed and the client is helped to make accurate causal attributions. Maladaptive beliefs are identified and disputed.

3 Successful encounters are identified in order to analyse the factors that have led to success and how these encounters differ from (2) above.

4 The client's range of options for handling situations differently is identified; similar situations are likely to be repeated and the client undertakes to try a modified approach. The various options can be rehearsed covertly or through role-play. The client may be offered advice as to how he/she can check out reality by seeking feedback from others rather than relying on presupposition.

5 The client reports back on the success or otherwise of the assignment, and the cycle is repeated.

There is a risk with this approach that issues relating to the past (such as the development of the problem, past trauma) or the future (such as where the client is heading) are neglected. In practice, these issues are often expressed in the course of discussing daily incidents, and in any case parts of a session or whole sessions can be devoted to them. In whatever way clients modify their social life, questions of value, personal philosophy and long-term aims are likely to arise. It is preferable to discuss these questions in the context of concrete choices rather than in the abstract.

Another potential disadvantage of focusing on day-to-day events is that systematic grading of tasks may prove difficult. The counsellor can dissuade a client from over-ambitious attempts to do things which are likely to prove distressing or disappointing. Conversely, simple routine activities, like going to a launderette, can be made more challenging by suggesting, for example, that the client attempt to strike up a conversation there. One client, an extremely isolated, unemployed man, suggested an assignment that was at the right level of difficulty for him. Although he had given up heavy drinking several years earlier, he started to attend meetings of Alcoholics Anonymous, where he met sympathetic people who befriended him. When a collaborative style is adopted, a client will usually be able to suggest ways of extending regular social activities that are meaningful and rewarding, as in this case.

Exploratory guided fantasy and covert rehearsal   Guided fantasy is a useful technique to gain information about the client's habitual reactions. It also provides an opportunity for covert rehearsal of alternative responses. It is less threatening than behaviour rehearsal through role-play, is highly flexible, and usually produces an unpremeditated response which is faithful to the client's usual style of interaction.

Illustration: A woman had difficulty in starting and maintaining intimate heterosexual relationships, and a guided fantasy (see chapter 6) was employed to clarify the reasons. She imaginatively involved herself in what had happened on a recent date. This revealed that the man she was with had been (according to her account) over-friendly, by taking her arm crossing the street and by holding her hand in the back of a taxi. A discussion of fantasy content allowed us to identify the assumptions she was making about the man's intentions, the degree of intimacy she really wanted, and her fears that she would be unable to control the level of intimacy expressed. The fantasy was changed to include slightly more intimate advances and she reported back her immediate reactions. These were strong and aggressive and so various options for curtailing the friend's advances were discussed and covertly rehearsed. She felt confident enough to put these into practice and was able to report back the following week that she had been assertive rather than aggressive in a similar situation. Feeling more in control, she was less anxious about what might happen on a date. A premature termination of the relationship was probably avoided.

Behaviour rehearsal and reverse role-play   Role-play is used to rehearse difficult social interactions that the client is reporting in the diary. It can also be useful to rehearse situations that are coming up in the near future. However, not all situations easily translate into role-play, for example the scenario described above. Some clients in any case refuse to comply with role-play but the method *does* have clear advantages in that it allows the counsellor to observe the client's behaviour at first hand.

Before attempting behaviour rehearsal, the client should be given a clear explanation of its purpose (assessment, skill acquisition or both) emphasizing that role-play is a safe and controlled way of exploring difficulties. The usual procedure is as follows:

1. The client outlines the social situation that is distressing or difficult (preferably based on a recent incident).
2. The counsellor engages the client in a role-play lasting no longer than a few minutes, following the outline provided. The client receives no instruction apart from playing his/her normal self.

3. The client is asked what he/she thought of the role-play, whether it reproduced the difficulty reasonably well, and to comment on the adequacy of their own performance and the outcome.

4. If the client does not spontaneously point out aspects that could be modified, the counsellor singles out one or two aspects on which it is intended to work (the amount of feedback on the role-play is limited to avoid overwhelming the client). Aspects of the role-play that were handled well by the client are praised.

5. The same scenario is repeated following a discussion of how the client (or counsellor) might play the scene differently. The counsellor might decide to model for the client how the situation could be handled differently, enabling the client to imitate either content or non-verbal aspects. Alternatively, the client is simply prompted by suggestion to re-enact the scene differently.

6. The client is again requested to comment, this time on whether the experience felt any different, whether the outcome had changed, and whether the new style of approaching the situation represents a satisfactory improvement. It is important that clients come to their own conclusion about the exercise and that all reservations and objections are taken up. However, the counsellor may suggest reruns which emphasize particular aspects, in the spirit of learning by experiment, even if the client feels they are out of character.

Role-play can be useful as a technique for identifying maladaptive beliefs. For example, a client may state that acting is false and morally objectionable. This may lead into a discussion of the way in which a person's social presentation does in fact differ across situations, and hence into an examination of assumptions about social expectations.

Reverse role-play This is a method for giving a client feedback on how he/she appears to others. The counsellor simulates as closely as possible the client's performance in a role-play. This gives the client an idea of what it feels like to be someone interacting with a person with his/her characteristics and how these could be changed to have a more socially rewarding effect. If sensitively managed, the client is motivated to try out a modified style of interaction when the role-play procedure is reversed back again.

Reverse role-play also provides an opportunity for the client to dispute his or her own maladaptive beliefs as played out by the counsellor.

Suggestions for further reading

For further discussion of worrying and stimulus control, see Borkovec et al. (1983, 1986) and Borkovec (1990). Problem-solving methods have been described by Goldfried and Davison (1976). The concept of core irrational beliefs (or dysfunctional assumptions) has been widely discussed in the literature on rational emotive therapy (e.g. Ellis and Harper, 1975; Dryden and DiGiuseppe, 1990; Warren and Zgourides, 1991) and on Beck's cognitive therapy (e.g. Beck et al., 1985; Blackburn and Davidson, 1990).

Relaxation has been the subject of many books and articles. Barber (1984) provides an integrative review. There are many treatment manuals, especially on progressive muscular relaxation (e.g. Bernstein and Borkovec, 1973). Benson (1976) and Borysenko (1988) are reasonably priced paperbacks for the non-specialist. Applied relaxation is described by Deffenbacher and Snyder (1981) and Ost (1987). For social anxiety see Butler (1985, 1989), Cheek et al. (1966), Hartman (1986), Heimberg et al. (1987) and Hope et al. (1989). Some popular guides to assertiveness training are Alberti and Emmons (1982), Dickson (1982) and Lange and Jakubowski (1976).

9

Overcoming Obstacles to Progress and Ending the Counselling Relationship

Some of the difficulties that commonly arise in working with anxiety problems can be identified but every client is unique and the reasons for an unsatisfactory outcome may be hard to specify. I will discuss potential difficulties at three phases of counselling – orientation, assessment and intervention, and then comment on the process of ending the counselling relationship.

Obstacles when orienting the client

Before any progress can be made at all, the client will want to be convinced that he/she has come to the right counsellor and is being offered an appropriate form of help. In addition to explaining the general approach (verbally and through suggestions for reading; see Appendices) the counsellor should offer to answer any questions the client may have. It is also helpful, and sometimes vital, to inform and educate family members or partners. The following obstacles may be encountered at this stage.

Client's focus on symptoms and their physical treatment

Clients who experience anxiety problems as physical symptoms and think they have a medical disorder pose several difficulties. The first is that physical factors may be contributing to the problem even if they are not its primary cause. The counsellor should ensure that the physical contribution is understood and should refer to a physician if doubt remains. It is not possible in every case to reach a firm conclusion about this: an open mind is the best policy. A client's view that medical factors are present should be respected even if no evidence can be produced to support it. When a client resists evidence showing an *absence* of a suspected physical disorder, the counsellor has little or no choice but to go along with the client, proceeding on whatever common ground is possible in the hope that this conviction will weaken, or express a more forceful opinion and risk the client's disengagement. A client is unlikely to be seeking counselling if he/she is convinced that the problem is entirely physical. Counselling can be presented as a means of exploring the psychological dimension, the client's collaboration being sought as a way of testing out the relevance and validity of psychological factors. Contextual and cognitive influences can often be demonstrated quite easily by means of behavioural tests, experiments with imagery, or diary recording (see chapter 7, illness fears).

Passivity

A set of attitudes which often accompany a view of anxiety as an illness is that of passivity in the hands of the 'expert'. The client expects to have the problem removed quickly and without discomfort. The grounds for this expectation should be thoroughly investigated rather than glossed over by accepting flattering comments such as 'I *know* you'll be able to help me.' If the client is unable to see that the expectation is unreasonable, a counsellor should clearly state that he/she can only point, not lead, the way, that progress is largely dependent on the client's own efforts, and that the process may well be long and arduous. If asked how long it will take to 'eliminate' the problem, it is usually best to state that hurrying the work is counterproductive but that some indication of progress should be evident in 3–5 sessions. At this point, it can be suggested that the situation is reviewed jointly. Some clients should be encouraged to rethink their request for counselling once they have fully understood what it entails. The time taken to orientate and prepare a reluctant or passive client is almost always time well spent.

Obstacles to an adequate assessment

The presence of one major anxiety problem should not blind the counsellor to the presence of other problems that could constitute obstacles to progress. These include physical disorders (see chapter 1) and other psychological difficulties. The following might be missed:

> another anxiety problem (e.g. social anxiety, blood phobia);
> hyperventilation syndrome (see chapter 7);
> other types of problem (e.g. unassertiveness, depressed mood or obsessive behaviour);
> relationship problems;
> unresolved bereavement or trauma;
> dependence on anti-anxiety medications, alcohol, or other substances.

Client's relationships to significant others

The problem may have arisen in the context of conflict or stress within a relationship. These difficulties may have resolved themselves by the time the client seeks help. Whether they have or not, the assumption should not be made automatically that an interpersonal conflict has 'caused' the anxiety problem and that this is what should be addressed first. It is equally likely that an anxiety problem gives rise to interpersonal difficulties. Counselling itself, if it encourages assertiveness or independence, will impact on the client's relationships too.

In any event, the counsellor may think it advisable (with the client's permission) to interview persons who are closely involved in the client's life. These interviews will normally be conducted jointly. The need to interview may arise in the following circumstances:

First, if it becomes clear in the assessment that a client's anxieties concern the behaviour of others (or their failure to behave in certain ways). Instead of responding constructively to the difficulty (by expressing grief, anger, resentment, guilt or self-assertion) the client attributes his/her emotional upset to 'anxiety'. For example, in the course of assessing a woman who was complaining of anxiety, careful questioning elicited the fact that she was angry with her husband who had attempted suicide some months earlier and was concerned that he was failing to deal with his own problems and letting his family down. Unfortunately, the spouse refused to attend with my client, who also stopped attending. She returned a few months later when the couple had started to live more harmoniously. By this time her complaints of anxiety had ceased and she was mainly sad and angry about other aspects of her life circumstances. For this client, there would have been little point in dealing with the 'anxiety problem' directly.

Second, in cases where the significant other denies any involvement with the client's problem or, if not denying it, refuses to collaborate, the counsellor can help him/her to reach a more satisfactory adjustment to an unsatisfactory situation. Diary recording of distress should reveal the way in which interpersonal factors influence the problem and how they might be resolved. When the client is being encouraged to act more assertively or relinquish dependencies (which is often the case) the client should be warned that changes of this kind are not without significant consequences, not all of which can be predicted. Ideally, the client is able to put the relationship on a different footing but this is not always possible. Dependent relationships with a parent, spouse or partner may be placed under considerable strain or may have to be temporarily or permanently broken off. Some clients are understandably reluctant to make changes in a relationship that threaten its existence. Some clients drop out of counselling for this reason. In some cases, the fear of greater independence is due to a realization that an alternative source of security (work, friendship, etc.) seems out of reach.

Third, when the client wants to involve people who are close to him/her in the intervention. The nature of the desired assistance can be explained and sought out in the course of a joint interview (see chapter 7, self-managed programmes). Some potential difficulties that arise when others are ostensibly collaborating are: sensitizing the client to a threat, offering conflicting advice, envy of the client's achievements, 'put down' when the client makes a small step towards improvement, and a client's fears about how a partner will react to change.

It is sometimes helpful to encourage the client to be open about the actual problem with people in general so that others are better informed and in a position to help. Discovering that other people have similar problems or fail to react negatively helps to remove the sense of shame that may attach to an anxiety problem.

Unresolved bereavement or trauma

The significance of a past trauma or bereavement may be missed because the client cannot access the memory, is unwilling to talk about it, or does not mention it because it seems unconnected to the anxiety problem. A counsellor should remain on the alert for causal antecedents of this kind and occasionally repeat questions such as 'Does this remind you of anything that has happened in the past?' The chief clues to an unresolved trauma are:

- intrusive thoughts or images (i.e. mental content that breaks into other activities and distracts attention). This might be revealed in the course of diary recording or the client can be asked to jot down intrusive thoughts that come to mind in a small notebook;
- during a session, noting signs of emotional distress such as strain in the voice, sudden changes of facial expression, or tears;
- a lack of emotional responsiveness in talking about certain issues (which the client might report as emotional numbness);
- minor avoidances such as not visiting certain places, not mentioning certain names, or leaving things associated with a dead person 'exactly as they were'.

If a past trauma is identified, it can be helpful for the client to relive the experience in fantasy and restructure the memory (see

'Suggestions for further reading' for examples of how this is done). This intervention may help the client overcome a current anxiety problem.

Dependence on anti-anxiety medications

The safety and wisdom of prescribing such medications has been seriously questioned recently by some sections of the medical community. Many clients are also now 'anti-drug'. Counsellors have inherited a legacy of clients who have been taking anti-anxiety medication for many years and are fearful of giving it up. Psychological, and in some cases physical, dependence has developed. The medication may act as a safety signal, without which the client lacks the confidence to face up to stressful situations (although simply carrying the drug may suffice for some clients). If physically dependent, the client experiences withdrawal effects (similar to reactions typical of anxiety) when an attempt is made to reduce the intake of the drug. If withdrawal effects are severe and constitute the main problem of the client, referral to a psychiatric specialist is advisable.

The main classes of anti-anxiety medication are benzodiazepines, antidepressants (tricyclics or monoamine oxidase inhibitors), and beta blockers. It is advisable to be well informed about the way these drugs are prescribed and to know their side-effects (see 'Suggested reading'). It is unfortunately the case that many of the clients prescribed these drugs have not been closely supervised by their physicians. An individual's sensitivity and tolerance of drugs varies widely, making it necessary to monitor side-effects and adjust dosages. Clients may not be taking drugs as prescribed, or even taking them at effective levels. Some drugs are prescribed to be taken 'as needed' and others at fixed intervals which should be adhered to. Some drugs such as certain benzodiazepines act quickly and have a short duration of action (a few hours). This can be an advantage for occasional use but could create a see-sawing level of distress when used chronically, leading to rapid psychological dependence. Tolerance for benzodiazepines develops over a matter of weeks and so some psychiatrists recommend short-term prescription only (at most a few months).

It is probably safe to assume that when a client has been on anti-anxiety medication for six months or more (some clients have been on it for decades) without significant benefit, a medication withdrawal programme should accompany counselling. The latter should always be conducted with the client's full consent and the collaboration of the prescriber. If the medication has clearly been beneficial, especially at the beginning, it is still advisable to seek a reduction, except in circumstances outlined below. There are several cautions. First, a withdrawal programme requires close monitoring and should be conducted over at least six weeks (for further guidance see 'Suggested reading'). Second, clients who suddenly become anti-drug (because of influences from the media or because they sense the counsellor's opposition to their use) may stop all drugs immediately, even medication that has been prescribed for conditions other than 'anxiety'. Third, withdrawal is likely to exacerbate an anxiety problem that has been suppressed by the drugs as well as lead to withdrawal side-effects. Fourth, for clients who are undergoing severe (but temporary) stress, it is probably safer to delay withdrawal until the period of stress is over. In all cases, the counsellor is guided by the client's confidence in undertaking a reduction and by how distressed the client feels (i.e. the combined withdrawal effects and 'rebound' anxiety).

Brief guidelines for the use and withdrawal of anti-anxiety drugs Identify the names of prescribed drugs, the amount prescribed, pattern of consumption, and any effect the client has noticed from changing the dosage. Monitor changes in the pattern of use.

Ensure that the client understands what he/she is taking and why.

Drugs that have been prescribed for occasional use may continue to be valuable in this way until the client is confident enough to dispense with them; for example some public performers use beta blockers to suppress heart pounding or motor tremor; intermittent insomnia may be helped by medication as severe lack of sleep increases vulnerability to stressors. A one-off use of a drug might help a client break through a barrier of fear in a particular situation such as a first flight in an aeroplane.

Chronic drug use may impede counselling if it suppresses emotions or blunts awareness. However, medication is rarely a *major* obstacle to counselling. Counselling can be initiated without insisting on prior withdrawal of all medication. As a client gains confidence in the benefits of counselling, the wish to cut down normally arises spontaneously. It is then a case of deciding which drug to reduce first (if several are prescribed) and to ensure that the reduction is gradual. Weekly monitoring is advisable. Special care should be taken with anti-depressants. These do not have noticeable short-term effects and a client might believe wrongly that they are ineffective. (Note that these drugs have been used for both their anti-anxiety and anti-depressant effects.) Some doctors will switch a client from a short-acting benzodiazepine to one with a longer half-life (or switch to a different type of drug) before starting a withdrawal programme.

Help the client to distinguish withdrawal side-effects from the re-emergence of an anxiety problem. Withdrawal effects such as insomnia, irritability, confusion and cramps should subside over the withdrawal period.

Apart from some notable exceptions, it has not been my experience that withdrawal from medication has posed major problems. In the exceptional case, referral to a psychiatrist is advisable.

Alcohol dependence

Clients who are addicted to alcohol (that is, experience withdrawal effects such as shaking, agitation, profuse sweating, fears and depression) should be referred to specialist agencies. Many anxious clients have a less serious drinking problem. They may experience hangovers but are not yet drinking to avoid withdrawal effects. Alcohol can relieve an anxiety problem in the short term (because it tends to depress cortical functions that mediate negative thoughts and social inhibitions) but there is normally a rebound tension, nervousness or restlessness that lasts for hours, days or even weeks. A regular drinker may not be aware of this until the amount of alcohol consumed is reduced. Alcohol therefore tends to make an anxiety problem worse over the longer term.

Whether a client opts for abstinence or a reduced intake of alcohol is largely a matter of preference. When drinking is clearly related to a stress or anxiety problem, the need to drink should reduce during the course of counselling. Control over drinking is often the most appropriate aim. A client should make known to others his/her intent to cut down and monitor consumption in the anxiety diary. An analysis of these records should point to sensible modifications of drinking behaviour: for example, deciding not to drink in certain company, arranging for others to limit the length of drinking, changing the amount and style of drinking. The diary should also reveal the way in which alcohol is used as a coping strategy. For further guidance on the management of problem drinking, see 'Suggested reading'.

Obstacles to the success of interventions

Even with the most careful assessment and well-thought-out inter-vention, progress through counselling is not always smooth. The following checklist is a prompt to explore some of the possible reasons for a lack of progress in counselling.

1. The client has not been fully prepared for the intervention or does not fully accept it; e.g. does not understand its rationale, has no faith in its efficacy, does not know what is required of him/her, views seeking help as a sign of personal weakness.

2. The client has unrealistic expectations of the intervention; e.g. expects more rapid change or expects the counsellor to take responsibility for change.

3. The counsellor fails to notice that the client is only superficially compliant (out of traditional deference to the 'expert' or through adopting a passively resistant style).

4. The counsellor does not adjust to the client's preferred pattern of communication; e.g. explains ideas in too simple or sophisticated a manner, jokes inappropriately, or is too dismissive of client's concerns.

5. The client undermines or discounts any sign of change. This may relate to unrealistic expectations or to dysfunctional assumptions of the type 'I have been too damaged by past events to be able to change'.

6. Insufficient attention has been paid to helping the client develop new goals or a more secure/satisfying lifestyle; that is, a stressful situation may be preferred to a possibly better but uncertain one, if the former offers at least some sources of security and safety.

7. There is a chronic source of stress, conflict or uncertainty in the client's life whose influence has been underestimated in the assessment. The influence may be that of preoccupying the client (so that mental resources are directed elsewhere) or of maintaining a high level of arousal which slows the rate of extinction/habituation during confrontational interventions. It may be advisable to switch the focus of counselling away from an anxiety problem on to solving a problem or helping the client make important life decisions.

8. The following problems may arise in a confrontational intervention:

- The situation that is confronted (real-life or symbolic) does not access significant (or the most significant) elements of an anxiety memory. The situation may signify threats that have not been identified.
- The counsellor proceeds too fast as a result of giving insufficient time to establishing trust and confidence or of failure to seek feedback from the client.
- The extinction/habituation effect fails to generalize to significant everyday situations, in which case the latter should be incorporated into the programme. Alternatively, aversive events in the

everyday situation (e.g. hostile reactions, performance failures) may be resensitizing the client.
- Confrontational practice is insufficiently regular, prolonged or systematic.
- The steps in the confrontational programme are not graded finely enough to allow a gradual build-up of confidence. The client is demotivated by being given overwhelmingly difficult tasks.
- The client confronts with an inappropriate mental set; e.g. avoids making full contact with the situation, perceives it as unreal, 'fights' tension or is unable to accept ('flow with') the discomfort that is experienced.
- Insufficient attention has been paid to consolidating progress (i.e. 'overlearning'), ensuring that the client can cope with challenging, but infrequently occurring, events that he/she is likely to encounter.

9. In restructuring beliefs and disputing assumptions, a lack of progress may reflect poor application of technique rather than any intrinsic deficiencies in the approach. Expert supervision is needed to acquire a high level of proficiency. The following difficulties may arise:

- The client has not been adequately prepared; e.g. in the collaborative nature of the enterprise or in reaching an understanding of the cognitive model.
- The client has not identified a problem for which the technique is appropriate.
- The counsellor tends to provide answers rather than allow the client to come to his/her own conclusions ('guided discovery').
- There is a tendency to focus too much on thinking and neglect problem solving and behavioural change.
- The session lacks structure and focus; attempts to deal with too many issues at once.
- There is a premature use of technique before the meaning of situations has been explored and thoughts/assumptions have been identified.
- The client is unable to identify thoughts/assumptions associated with an anxiety problem despite reasonable efforts to do so; the relevant memories may be too distressing, thoughts that seem ridiculous or shameful may be concealed, the connections between cognition and emotion may be too obscure for either the client or counsellor to discover.
- The counsellor does not sufficiently repeat the process of

disputing the evidence for an irrational belief or the client does not rehearse it in the problem situation.
- Significant others strengthen the client's unrealistic appraisal of their own abilities or the severity of a threat.

10. There is a repeated lack of compliance with homework tasks. The following reasons should be considered:

- The client was not sufficiently prepared; the tasks were too difficult and/or there was too much to remember.
- The client could not really see the point of doing the tasks; they were seen as irrelevant.
- A task has brought to light problems or negative thoughts that the client had not anticipated.
- The client's situation has changed; e.g. extra demands have reduced the time available.
- The client is expressing through non-compliance an opinion on the therapeutic relationship or negative expectations of counselling.

Bringing counselling to an end

In chapter 3 I argued for making the contract with the client open-ended but subject to several constraints mentioned there. An exception to the general rule of an open-ended contract may have to be made when the client's anxiety problem directly concerns fears of being negatively evaluated, rejected or 'unloved'. Termination of counselling may be construed as confirmation of these fears. A hint that ending the counselling will be difficult for a client can usually be gleaned in the first assessment session. The response to previous professional contacts is often informative. A request to know 'how much' counselling is available may also be significant in this respect. For this group of clients, it is advisable to arrange a fixed-length contract and, as it expires, to remind the client how many sessions are left. A new contract can be arranged if this seems appropriate. One style of counselling would utilize the client's dependency on the counsellor and anxiety about ending the relationship as an opportunity for cognitive analysis of the problem. However, this strategy would focus attention on the client–counsellor relationship rather than on events in the client's life. There is a possibility that it would jeopardize the open, collaborative style of communication characteristic of the cognitive-behavioural approach. In other words, although such feelings would be openly accepted they would not normally be a vehicle for the application of techniques.

A point will, of necessity, be reached at which counselling is 'officially' terminated, usually when it becomes obvious to the client that the major problems have been resolved. Less satisfactorily, the counsellor will prepare the client for ending the relationship when it is clear that no further progress seems possible. The counsellor makes known these views as early as possible and analyses the reasons for lack of progress with the client, leading perhaps to a last attempt to intervene in a modified way. Assuming that a particular obstacle has been identified, a counsellor may wish to suggest that when the client's circumstances have changed or when the client feels differently disposed to the approach that has been offered, a further contact can be made. In practice, many clients drop out of counselling before the opportunity for this sort of discussion arises. It is not helpful to impute blame to either party and the counsellor may have to admit frankly that he/she has run out of ideas. Suggestions for alternative forms of help can be made.

In the happier case that the problem is resolved, the last session is a review of what has been achieved. If future difficulties are anticipated, the means of dealing with them are discussed and, if necessary, rehearsed. Most clients appreciate a contact telephone number in case of unexpected problems, and they rarely abuse this facility.

A follow-up session is arranged at an interval that matches the client's degree of confidence in being able to cope (e.g. 1–4 months). The purpose of following up the client is to ensure that change has consolidated. If it has not, or the client is reporting new difficulties, the position may be improved by timely action.

Suggestions for further reading

Obstacles to progress have been discussed in a general way by Emmelkamp and Bouman (1991). Chambless and Goldstein (1981) consider the relationship aspects of anxiety and phobia in some depth. For bereavement and trauma, see Ramsay (1979), Steketee and Foa (1987) and Worden (1983). A simple but informative account of anti-anxiety medications has been given by Greist et al. (1966), who advocate their use. For advice on withdrawal of anti-anxiety medication see Trickett (1986). A useful self-help guide to the reduction of problem drinking has been written by Robertson and Heather (1986).

Appendix A

Source Materials: Questionnaires and Books for the Lay Person

Questionnaires

Phobias
The fear questionnaire (Marks and Mathews, 1979)
The fear survey schedule (Wolpe and Lang, 1964)

Trait measures of anxiety and depression
State-Trait Anxiety Inventory (Spielberger et al., 1970)
Leeds scale for the assessment of anxiety and depression (Snaith et al., 1976)
Zung self-rating anxiety scale (Zung, 1979)
Cognitive and somatic anxiety questionnaire (Schwartz et al., 1978)
Beck Depression Inventory (Beck et al., 1961)

'Fear of Fear'
The body sensations questionnaire and the agoraphobic cognitions questionnaire (Chambless et al., 1984)
Anxiety sensitivity index (Reiss et al., 1986)

Measures of avoidance
The mobility inventory for agoraphobia (Chambless et al., 1985)

Social anxiety, shyness and assertiveness
Social avoidance and distress scale (Watson and Friend, 1969)
Negative evaluation scale (Watson and Friend, 1969)
Stanford shyness inventory (Zimbardo, 1977)
Rathus assertiveness schedule (Rathus, 1973)

Measures of irrational thinking
The belief scale (Malouff and Schutte, 1986)

Explanatory booklets and books

On conquering or coping with fear and anxiety
Overcoming Agoraphobia: Conquering Fear of the Outside World (Goldstein, 1988)
Agoraphobia: Nature and Treatment (Mathews et al., 1981: Patient's manuals, pp. 160–205)
Living with Fear (Marks, 1980)
Fighting Fear: the Eight-Week Program for Treating Your Own Fears (Neuman, 1985)
Peace from Nervous Suffering (Weekes, 1972)

On cognitive therapy principles
'Coping with anxiety' (in Beck et al. (1985), Appendix 1, pp. 315–22)
Coping with Depression (Blackburn, 1987)
Feeling Good: the New Mood Therapy (Burns, 1980)

Appendix B

Handout on Anxiety Problems

This handout is for new clients and is intended to orient them to the theoretical rationales and interventions described in this manual. It is part of the preparation phase of counselling and can be photocopied and given out in advance and used to prompt a client to ask questions.

Anxiety problems and how they can be helped by cognitive-behavioural counselling

This handout explains the cognitive-behavioural approach to anxiety problems and the sort of counselling you are likely to receive. Everyone is unique and so not everything that is written below will apply to you.

What counselling offers you
All of us experience anxiety at one time or another but it affects people in many different ways. An *anxiety problem* is a more severe form of *normal anxiety*. It is more intense or it is like a strong habit that is difficult to break. Counselling will help you to find out how your anxiety has developed into a problem that is interfering in your life. It will also show you how *you, yourself* can overcome it. An anxiety problem is not a medical illness or mental disorder. It is related to what has happened to you, to the stresses you face, to how you think of yourself, and to fears you may have about yourself or your future. This may not be obvious to you now but it should become so during the course of counselling.

You may always have thought of yourself as a 'worrier' or a 'nervous person'. Counselling will not change you into a completely different person. Some degree of anxiety and nervousness is normal and affects us all. Some people are certainly more prone to it than others. In counselling, we are concerned with anxiety that is *excessive and unreasonable*. In particular, the counsellor will be concerned to help you find out whether your anxiety problem is related to underlying beliefs about harm (or even just the image of something frightening), of which you are not, at the moment, fully aware. This form of counselling assumes that what you *think* about a situation affects the way you *feel* about it. Sometimes it is the effects of anxiety itself that you fear. For example, 'I will make a fool of myself if I have a panic' or 'My future will be ruined if I can't stop my hands from shaking'.

Some typical anxiety problems
In many anxiety problems your mind and body react as if you are facing an immediate danger or harm. The reactions are the same as if you were facing an actual danger, such as a street mugger, or a severe stress. The effects can be strong and overwhelming and so you may feel that there is something seriously wrong with your mind or body. This is not the case. The reactions of your mind and body are part of its normal functioning. They focus the mind on the danger to be dealt with and prepare the body for vigorous action. In the case of an anxiety problem, the thing you are responding to may be the memory of a past trauma, or something that you especially hate, such as spiders, or something that you worry might happen in the future, like failing at something or getting ill. As already mentioned, the reactions to anxiety itself may be feared. For example, you might imagine yourself being unable to speak just as you stand up to talk to an audience. The following are some typical anxiety problems. They may not be present in your particular case:

– mind going blank, not able to concentrate;
– worrying thoughts or unpleasant memories intruding into your mind;
– intense dislike or fear of some situations and therefore avoidance of them (e.g. talking to a stranger, having an injection);
– 'panic attacks' coming out of the blue; worrying that one will strike you without warning;
– unpleasant bodily sensations (e.g. sweats, heart pounding, muscle tension);
– muscle twitches or cramps.

What will happen in counselling?
The first stage is to find out more about your anxiety problem, what is triggering it, and what other stresses you face in your life. It is important for you to discover how you are interpreting situations and what you think of your own abilities to cope with an anxiety problem. The counsellor helps you to find this out for yourself – through questioning but also through imagining

situations or by doing things that make you anxious. You will probably be asked to keep a diary record of the times that you are anxious week by week. This will be discussed in the sessions so that you reach a better understanding of your problem.

The second stage helps you develop the skills and confidence to face up to situations (including imaginary ones) that distress you. This is always done in a gradual way with your full collaboration in finding the best way to do it. In addition to working on this in a session, the counsellor is likely to suggest tasks for you to carry out between sessions. Again, these tasks are worked out with you. At the same time, the counsellor will help you to examine what it is that makes the situation frightening – how you are thinking about it or your own abilities to deal with it. For example, are your beliefs about it based on good evidence? Are the things that you fear likely to happen? Are you underestimating your own abilities? You will be shown how to examine these thoughts yourself. You will not change the way you think simply by being told something by your counsellor. You will need to convince yourself first. You will discover the basis for your beliefs by being shown how to question your own evidence or by doing something in a different way and discovering the consequences.

In addition, you will discuss with the counsellor other aspects of your life in which, for example, you are facing up to difficulties in relationships, making major decisions, or coping with a stress like looking after an elderly relative. The purpose here is to help you resolve these difficulties in the best possible way so as to leave you with the energy and resources to deal with the anxiety problem that is affecting you.

The success of this form of counselling ultimately depends on your decision to face up to anxieties and your willingness to learn from the methods the counsellor suggests. Nobody can solve another's problems directly unless it is something like being without a home or money. The counsellor can only show you how to go about learning and point to ways of getting around a position in which you have got stuck. The counsellor will expect you to give feedback on what you think of the sessions and to say when you sense there is a lack of communication.

Cognitive-behavioural counselling is not normally a very lengthy form of help. It will take months rather than years. The sessions are likely to be frequent at first (say weekly), then the space between them will get longer as you begin to resolve your problem. You may of course continue to benefit from seeing your counsellor occasionally after the main sessions have come to an end. Problems may arise that you hadn't anticipated or a crisis might set you back. The counselling that is offered to you is not a 'quick fix' solution. Through overcoming your problem you will learn ways of dealing with other problems that are bound to arise, as they do in anyone's life. What you learn should be useful to you for the rest of your life.

References

Alberti, R. E. and M. E. Emmons (1982) *Your Perfect Right*, 4th edn. San Luis Obispo, CA: Impact.

Baker, R. (ed.) (1989) *Panic Disorder: Theory Research and Therapy*. Chichester: John Wiley.

Barber, T. X. (1984) 'Hypnosis, deep relaxation, and active relaxation: data, theory and clinical applications', in R. L. Woolfolk and P. M. Lehrer (eds), *Principles and Practice of Stress Management*. New York: Guilford. pp. 142–87.

Barker, P. J. (1985) *Patient Assessment in Psychiatric Nursing*. London: Croom Helm.

Barlow, D. (1988) *Anxiety and its Disorders*. New York: Guilford.

Barlow, D. and J. A. Cerny (1988) *Psychological Treatment of Panic*. New York: Guilford.

Beck, A. T., C. H. Ward, M. Mendelsohn, J. Mock and J. Erbaugh (1961) 'An inventory for measuring depression: psychometric properties', *Archives of General Psychiatry*, 4: 561–71.

Beck, A. T., G. Emery and R. Greenberg (1985) *Anxiety Disorder and Phobias: a Cognitive Perspective*. New York: Basic Books.

Benson, H. (1976) *The Relaxation Response*. London: Collins.

Bernstein, D. A. and T. D. Borkovec (1973) *Progressive Relaxation Training*. Champaign, IL: Research Press.

Blackburn, I. (1987) *Coping with Depression*. Edinburgh: Chambers.

Blackburn, I. and K. Davidson (1990) *Cognitive Therapy for Depression and Anxiety*. Oxford: Blackwell.

Borkovec, T. D. and J. Inz (1990) 'The nature of worry in generalised anxiety disorder: a predominance of thought activity', *Behaviour Research and Therapy*, 28: 153–8.

Borkovec, T. D., L. Wilkinson, R. Folensbee, and C. Lerman (1983) 'Stimulus control applications to the treatment of worry', *Behaviour Research and Therapy*, 21: 247–51.

Borkovec, T. D., T. Pruzinsky and R. Metzger (1986) 'Anxiety, worry, and the self', in L.M. Hartman and K. R. Blankstein (eds), *Perception of Self in Emotional Disorder*. New York: Plenum. pp. 219–57.

Borysenko, J. (1988) *Minding the Body, Mending the Mind*. London: Bantam Books.

Burns, D. D. (1980) *Feeling Good: the New Mood Therapy*. New York: New American Library.

Butler, G. (1985) 'Exposure as a treatment for social phobia: some instructive difficulties', *Behaviour Research and Therapy*, 23: 651–7.

Butler, G. (1989) 'Issues in the application of cognitive behavioural strategies to the treatment of social phobia', *Clinical Psychology Review*, 9: 91–106.

Chambless, D. L. and A. J. Goldstein (1981) 'Clinical treatment of agoraphobia', in M. Mavissakalian and D. H. Barlow (eds), *Phobia: Psychological and Pharmacological Treatment*. New York: Guilford. pp. 103–44.

Chambless, D. L., G. C. Caputo, P. Bright and R. Gallagher (1984) 'Assessment of fear in agoraphobics: the body sensations questionnaire and the agoraphobic cognitions questionnaire', *Journal of Consulting and Clinical Psychology*, 52: 1090–7.

Chambless, D. L., G. C. Caputo, S. E. Jasin, E. J. Gracely and C. Williams (1985) 'The mobility inventory for agoraphobia', *Behaviour Research and Therapy*, 23: 35–44.

Cheek, J. M., L. A. Melchior and A. M. Carpentieri (1986) 'Shyness and self-concept', in L. M. Hartman and K. R. Blankstein (eds), *Perception of Self in Emotional Disorder and Psychotherapy*. New York: Plenum. pp. 113–27.

Clark, D. M. (1986) 'A cognitive approach to panic', *Behaviour Research and Therapy*, 24: 461–70.

Clark, D. and A. T. Beck (1988) 'Cognitive approaches', in C. Last and M. Hersen (eds), *Handbook of Anxiety Disorders*. New York: Pergamon.

Clark, D. M. and P. M. Salkovskis (1992) *Cognitive Therapy for Panic and Hypochondriasis*. Oxford: Pergamon.

Deffenbacher, J. L. and A. L. Snyder (1981) 'Anxiety', in J. L. Shelton and R. L. Levy (eds), *Behavioral Assignments and Treatment Compliance*. Champaign, IL: Research Press. pp. 93–110.

Dickson, A. (1982) *A Woman in Your Own Right*. London: Quartet.

Dryden, W. and R. DiGiuseppe (1990) *A Primer on Rational Emotive Therapy*. Champaign, IL: Research Press.

Ellis, A. and R. A. Harper (1975) *A New Guide to Rational Living*. North Hollywood, CA: Wilshire.

Emmelkamp, P. M. G. (1982) *Phobic and Obsessive-Compulsive Disorders: Theory, Research and Practice*. New York: Plenum.

Emmelkamp, P. M. G. (1982) 'In vivo treatment of agoraphobia', in D. L. Chambless and A. J. Goldstein (eds), *Agoraphobia: Multiple Perspectives on Theory and Treatment*. New York: Wiley.

Emmelkamp, P. M. G. and T. K. Bouman (1991) 'Psychological approaches to the difficult patient', in J. R. Walker, G. R. Norton and C. A. Ross (eds), *Panic Disorder and Agoraphobia*. Pacific Grove, CA: Brooks/Cole. pp. 398–430.

Foa, E. and M. J. Kozak (1986) 'Emotional processing of fear: exposure to corrective information', *Psychological Bulletin*, 99: 20–35.

Goldfried, M. R. (1986) 'Self-control skills for the treatment of anxiety disorders', in B. F. Shaw, Z. V. Segel, T. M. Vallis and F. E. Cashman (eds), *Anxiety Disorders: Psychological and Biological Perspectives*. New York: Plenum. pp. 165–76.

Goldfried, M. R. and G. C. Davison (1976) *Clinical Behavior Therapy*. New York: Holt, Rinehart & Winston.

Goldstein, A. (1988) *Overcoming Agoraphobia: Conquering Fear of the Outside World*, New York: Viking Penguin.

Greist, J. H., J. W. Jefferson and I. M. Marks (1986) *Anxiety and its Treatment*. Washington, DC: American Psychiatric Press.

Hartman, L. M. (1986) 'Social anxiety, problem drinking, and self-awareness', in L. M. Hartman and K. R. Blankstein (eds), *Perception of Self in Emotional*

Disorder and Psychotherapy. New York: Plenum. pp. 265–81.

Hawton, K., P. M. Salkovskis, J. Kirk and D. M. Clark (1989) *Cognitive Behaviour Therapy for Psychiatric Problems: a Practical Guide*. Oxford: Oxford Medical Publications.

Heimberg, R. G., C. S. Dodge and R. E. Becker (1987) 'Social phobia', in L. Michelson and L. M. Ascher (eds), *Anxiety and Stress Disorders: Cognitive Behavioral Assessment and Treatment*. New York: Guilford Press. pp. 280–309.

Himadi, W. G. (1987) 'Safety signals and agoraphobia', *Journal of Anxiety Disorders*, 1: 345–60.

Hope, D. A., D. A. Gansler and R. G. Heimberg (1989) 'Attentional focus and causal attributions in social phobia', *Clinical Psychology Review*, 9: 49–60.

Jacob, R., S. O. Lilienfeld, J. Furman, J. D. Durrant and S. M. Turner (1989) 'Panic disorder with vestibular dysfunction: further clinical observations and description of space and motion phobia stimuli', *Journal of Anxiety Disorders*, 3: 117–30.

Kirk, J. (1989) 'Cognitive behavioural assessment', in K. Hawton, P. M. Salkovskis, J. Kirk and D. M. Clark (eds), *Cognitive Behaviour Therapy for Psychiatric Problems: A Practical Guide*. Oxford: Oxford Medical Publications. pp. 13–51.

Lange, A. and P. Jakubowski (1976) *Responsible Assertive Behavior: Cognitive-Behavioral Procedures for Trainers*. Champaign, IL: Research Press.

Last, C. and M. Hersen (eds) (1988) *Handbook of Anxiety Disorders*. New York: Pergamon.

Ley, R. (1985) 'Blood, breath and fears: a hyperventilation theory of panic attacks and agoraphobia', *Clinical Psychology Review*, 5: 271–85.

Malouff, J. M. and N. S. Schutte (1986) 'Development and validation of a measure of irrational belief', *Journal of Consulting and Clinical Psychology*, 54: 860–2.

Marks, I.M. (1980) *Living with Fear*. New York: McGraw-Hill.

Marks, I.M. (1987) *Fears, Phobias, and Rituals*. New York: Oxford University Press.

Marks, I. M. and A. M. Mathews (1979) 'Brief standard self-rating for phobic patients', *Behaviour Research and Therapy*, 17: 263–7.

Mathews, A. M., M. G. Gelder and D. W. Johnston (1981) *Agoraphobia: Nature and Treatment*. New York: Guilford.

McCue, E. C. and P. A. McCue (1984) 'Organic and hyperventilatory causes of anxiety-type symptoms', *Behavioural Psychotherapy*, 12: 308–17.

McNally, R. J. (1990) 'Psychological approaches to panic disorders: a review', *Psychological Bulletin*, 108: 403–19.

Michelson, L. and L. M. Ascher (eds) (1987) *Anxiety and Stress Disorders*. New York: Guilford.

Neuman, F. (1985) *Fighting Fear: the Eight-Week Program for Treating Your Own Fears*. New York: Bantam.

Ost, L. G. (1987) 'Applied relaxation: description of a coping technique and review of controlled studies', *Behaviour Research and Therapy*, 25: 397–409.

Rachman, S. (1984) 'Agoraphobia: a safety-signal perspective', *Behaviour Research and Therapy*, 22: 59–70.

Rachman, S. (1990) *Fear and Courage*, 2nd edn. New York: Freeman.

Rachman, S. and J. Maser (eds) (1988) *Panic: Psychological Perspectives*. Hillsdale, NJ: Erlbaum.

Ramsay, R. (1979) 'Bereavement: a behavioural treatment of pathological grief', in

P. O. Sjoden, S. Bates and W. S. Docken (eds), *Trends in Behavior Therapy*. New York: Academic Press.

Rathus, S. A. (1973) 'A 30-item schedule for assessing assertive behaviour', *Behavior Therapy*, 4: 398–406.

Reiss, S., R. A. Peterson, D. M. Gursky and R. J. McNally (1986) 'Anxiety sensitivity, anxiety frequency, and the prediction of fearfulness', *Behaviour Research and Therapy*, 24: 1–8.

Robertson, I. and N. Heather (1986) *Let's Drink to Your Health: a Self-Help Guide to Sensible Drinking*. Leicester: British Psychological Society.

Schwartz, G. E., R. J. Davidson and D. J. Coleman (1978) 'Patterning of cognitive and somatic processes in the self-regulation of anxiety: effects of meditation versus exercise', *Psychosomatic Medicine*, 40: 321–8.

Smail, D. (1984) Illusion and Reality. London: J. M. Dent.

Snaith, R. P., C. W. K. Bridges and M. Hamilton (1976) 'The Leeds scale for the assessment of anxiety and depression', *British Journal of Psychiatry*, 128: 156–65.

Spielberger, C. D., R. R. Gorsuch and R. E. Lushene (1970) *State-Trait Anxiety Inventory Test Manual for Form X*. Palo Alto, CA: Consulting Psychologists Press.

Steketee, G. and E. B. Foa (1987) 'Rape victims: post-traumatic stress responses and their treatment: a review of the literature', *Journal of Anxiety Disorders*, 1: 69–86.

Trickett, S. (1986) *Coming Off Tranquillizers and Sleeping Pills*. Wellingborough, Northants: Thorsons.

Trower, P., A. Casey and W. Dryden (1988) *Cognitive Behavioural Counselling in Action*. London: Sage.

Tuma, A. H. and J. D. Maser (eds) (1985) *Anxiety and the Anxiety Disorders*. Hillsdale, NJ: Erlbaum.

Walker, J. R., R. Norton and C. A. Ross (1991) *Panic Disorder and Agoraphobia: a Comprehensive Guide for the Practitioner*. Pacific Grove, CA: Brooks/Cole.

Warren, R. and G. D. Zgourides (1991) *Anxiety Disorders: a Rational-Emotive Perspective*. New York: Pergamon.

Warwick, H. M. E. and P. M. Salkovskis (1990) 'Hypochondriasis', *Behaviour Research and Therapy*, 28: 105–17.

Watson, D. and R. Friend (1969) 'Measurement of social evaluative anxiety', *Journal of Consulting and Clinical Anxiety*, 33: 448–57.

Watts, F. N. (1979) 'Habituation model of systematic desensitisation', *Psychological Bulletin*, 86: 627–37.

Weekes, C. (1972) *Peace from Nervous Suffering*. London: Angus & Robertson.

Weekes, C. (1977) *Simple Effective Treatment of Agoraphobia*. London: Angus & Robertson.

Williams, S. L. (1990) 'Guided mastery treatment of agoraphobia: beyond stimulus exposure', in M. Hersen, R. M. Eisler and P. M. Miller (eds), *Progress in Behavior Modification*, Vol. 25. Newbury Park, CA: Sage. pp. 119–51.

Wilson, G. T. (1986) 'Psychosocial treatment of anxiety disorders', in B. F. Shaw, Z. V. Segal, T. M. Vallis and F. E. Cashman (eds), *Anxiety Disorders: Psychological and Biological Perspectives*. New York: Plenum. pp. 149–60.

Wolpe, J. and P. J. Lang (1964) 'A fear survey schedule for use in behaviour therapy', *Behaviour Research and Therapy*, 2: 27–30.

Worden, J. W. (1983) *Grief Counselling and Grief Therapy*. London: Tavistock.

Zimbardo, P. G. (1977) *Shyness: What It Is and What To Do About It*. Reading, MA: Addison Wesley.

Zung, W. W. K. (1979) 'A rating instrument for anxiety disorders', *Psychosomatics*, 12: 371–9.

Index